EARLY WORKS OF
EDNA ST. VINCENT MILLAY

EARLY WORKS OF EDNA ST. VINCENT MILLAY
Selected Poetry and Three Plays

EDNA ST. VINCENT MILLAY

INTRODUCTION BY
STACY CARSON HUBBARD

BARNES & NOBLE
NEW YORK

THE BARNES & NOBLE
LIBRARY OF ESSENTIAL READING

Introduction and Suggested Reading © 2006
by Barnes & Noble, Inc.

Originally published between 1917 and 1921

This 2006 edition published by Barnes & Noble, Inc.

ISBN-13: 978-0-7607-8078-7
ISBN-10: 0-7607-8078-1

Printed and bound in the United States of America

1 3 5 7 9 10 8 6 4 2

CONTENTS

INTRODUCTION

HER VOICE WAS, BY ALL ACCOUNTS, THRILLING. WHETHER ONSTAGE with the Provincetown Players, on tour reciting her poems to packed auditoriums, or reading on weekly radio broadcasts during the 1930s, Edna St. Vincent Millay's rich contralto had a galvanizing effect on audiences. The critic Louis Untermeyer remembered it "like the sound of the ax on fresh wood," and Edmund Wilson recalled that when she read, "the company hushed and listened as people do to music."[1] Coupled with the already dramatic qualities of her poems—their high romantic passions, their startling frankness about sexual matters, their wry humor—and her striking physical presence, this voice helped to make Millay one of the first celebrity artists of the twentieth century, someone whose popularity was rivaled only by the film stars emerging on the scene at about the same time. In our own era, we might liken Millay to Madonna. Like Madonna's, Millay's identity and style were hard to pin down. The power of her personal presence and the emotive force of her language could make her poetry seem utterly sincere and disturbingly intimate. Contrarily, her heightened rhetoric, allusions to earlier literature, and multiple personae could suggest the most studied of performances. In the almost one hundred years since her poetry first came to public notice, Millay has been praised and condemned for both qualities.

This volume reprints Millay's early poems and plays, published between 1917 and 1921, just as she was first "danc[ing] like a Bomb, abroad"[2] (to borrow a phrase from Emily Dickinson). These texts helped to create the famous figure of the "girl poet," Edna Millay, and to shape the terms by which her work would be received for years to come.

Edna St. Vincent Millay was born on February 22nd, 1892, in Rockland, Maine, to Cora Buzzell Millay and Henry Tolman Millay. She acquired her middle name from St. Vincent's Hospital, where her maternal uncle had recently been treated, and throughout her life she was known to friends and family as "Vincent" rather than Edna. Along with her two younger sisters, Millay was encouraged by her mother to pursue literary and musical studies (one sister became an actress, the other a poet). When she was eight, Millay's parents divorced and she moved with her mother and sisters to Camden, Maine, where the girls were left alone for long periods of time while Cora Millay supported them by working as a traveling nurse. Much of Millay's early life reads like a version of *Little Women*: a missing father, a beloved but often absent mother, talented and affectionate sisters overburdened by domestic duties while dreaming of bigger things. Bigger things began to happen for "Vincent" Millay at an early age. She published her first poem in *St. Nicholas Magazine* for children (where Louisa May Alcott had also often published) when she was fourteen. In 1912, when she was twenty, Millay's mother encouraged her to enter a poetry contest sponsored by *The Lyric Year*, which promised publication to the best one hundred poems and cash prizes to the top three. Millay's submission, "Renascence," took fourth place, but the anthology's publication gave rise to a general outcry at Millay's not having received top honors. The subsequent notoriety and shows of support from more established poets doubtless benefited Millay more than the prize would have done. She was hailed as a poetic prodigy and "Renascence" was lauded for its spiritual freshness and dramatic power.

This youthful triumph led to a scholarship at Vassar College, where Millay received a broad education in classical and modern languages and distinguished herself as a poet, playwright, actress, and flouter of the college rules (she was almost prevented from graduating when she spent a weekend away from campus without permission). After taking her degree in 1917, Millay moved with her sister Norma to Greenwich Village, at the time a vortex of artistic experiment, radical politics, and free love. There, she supported herself by acting with the Provincetown Players and the Playwright's Theatre and publishing satirical prose in *Ainslee's* (a popular periodical) and *Vanity Fair* under the pen name Nancy Boyd. Her circle of acquaintances and lovers included many famous names of the period: Floyd Dell, John Reed, Max and Crystal Eastman, Elinor Wylie, Alfred Kreymborg, Eugene O'Neill, and Edmund Wilson. With her publication in 1920 of *A Few Figs from Thistles* (in which she famously claimed that her "candle burns at both ends"), the fantastic success of her anti-war play, *Aria da Capo,* the same year, and her public support of feminist and radical causes (such as the campaign to save Sacco and Vanzetti from execution), Millay became a symbol of feminism and youthful rebellion in the post-war period. In 1923, after traveling and living in Europe for two years, Millay returned to America to become the first woman to receive the Pulitzer Prize (for *A Few Figs, The Ballad of the Harp-Weaver,* and eight of her sonnets). Also in 1923, she married Eugen Boissevain, a Dutch importer and widower of the famous suffragist, Inez Milholland, and together they relocated to a farm near the Berkshires, which they named Steepletop. Among Millay's most well-respected works are *Second April* (1921), an opera entitled *The King's Henchmen* (staged to great acclaim by the Metropolitan Opera in 1927), the sonnet sequence *Fatal Interview (1931),* an experimental play entitled *Conversation at Midnight* (1937), and a final posthumous volume of poems, *Mine the Harvest* (1954), which contains some of her most memorable sonnets. *Make Bright the Arrows* (1940), and a radio play, *The Murder of Lidice* (1942), both written in support of the war effort, were, by Millay's own admission, more propaganda than poetry, and led to a steep decline in her reputation. After many years of debilitating illness, pain from an injury suffered in a car accident, and drug and alcohol dependency, Millay died in a fall down the stairs at Steepletop on October 19, 1950, at the age of fifty-eight.

"Renascence," the poem which launched Millay's career in 1912, and which reached an even broader audience when it was reprinted in *Renascence and Other Poems* in 1917, is still perhaps Millay's most well-known work (though in later years she lamented this fact). It sets in motion the central themes of her early work. Like many of Dickinson's poems, "Renascence" speaks from the grave, pitting the small self with its limitless imagination against an overwhelming world and an unfathomable deity. The poem begins with its speaker firmly bound by the physical world:

> All I could see from where I stood
> Was three long mountains and a wood;
> I turned and looked another way,
> And saw three islands and a bay.
>
> . . .
>
> Over these things I could not see;
> These were the things that bounded me.
>
> . . . .
>
> And all at once things seemed so small
> My breath came short, and scarce at all.

The feeling of claustrophobia is palpable, and it intensifies as the speaker reaches out to touch the sky, only to find that such contact brings the sky down upon her in a kind of living burial: "I screamed, and—lo!—Infinity / Came down and settled over me." The speaker is shown an image of "Immensity," made to hear the "ticking of Eternity," and suffers as her own all the pain and guilt of a sinning world until she is glad to be freed of such sympathy through death. In "Renascence," overreaching is punished by a nightmarish access to experience of cosmic dimensions and the only escape from such overwhelming knowledge is the assertion of desire and will—here, in the form of a prayer that God will return her to life so that she may once again witness the wonders of nature. The poem ends with a moral about the necessity of the self's being equal to—or, as Whitman might say, "tallying"—the world:

> The world stands out on either side
> No wider than the heart is wide;
> Above the world is stretched the sky—
> No higher than the soul is high.
>
> . . .
>
> The soul can split the sky in two,

And let the face of God shine through.
But East and West will pinch the heart
Than can not keep them pushed apart;
And he whose soul is flat—the sky
Will cave in on him by and by.

The theme of the poem is, as in all of Millay's poetry, experience—a plea on behalf of "living large." Though "Renascence" was received by many as a religious or visionary poem, God's presence is less instrumental in its narrative than the speaker's own power to push back against the potentially crushing weight of worldly knowledge. Its voice is that of the repressed child reclaiming her birthright of egotism, asserting her appetite for experience. And the process the poem describes is precisely the process that the poem set in motion for its young author: it unburied her. From a childhood of impoverished duty and rural obscurity, Millay was suddenly thrust onto center stage of a very wide and rather unruly world. By the time *Renascence and Other Poems* appeared, Americans were embroiled in World War I, and Millay's youthful allegory of struggle and rebirth spoke to the hopes of a generation hungry for vital experience in the face of suffering and death.

The themes of experience, self-assertion, and naïve wonder which characterize its title poem are continued in several other poems in *Renascence,* such as "God's World" ("Oh world, I cannot hold thee close enough!") and "Afternoon on a Hill." Poems such as "Interim," "The Suicide," and "The Shroud" develop the elegiac note that would form a prominent strand of Millay's poetry throughout her career. "Witch-Wife" and "Bluebeard" illustrate the influence of fairy tales, especially on Millay's depictions of relations between men and women. As became her habit, Millay closed the volume with a cluster of sonnets (and this is notable for the way it gives precedence to the ballads and free-verse poems, using the more tightly crafted sonnets as a kind of *envoi*). One of these, in particular, demonstrates the skill with which, from early on, Millay could loosen the sonnet's form to accommodate narrative and modernize it with gritty details and vernacular phrasing. It also shows how much emotional power she could wring from understatement, when she chose to use it.

If I should learn, in some quite casual way,
That you were gone, not to return again—
Read from the back-page of a paper, say,
Held by a neighbor on a subway train,
How at the corner of this avenue
And such a street (so are the papers filled)
A hurrying man, who happened to be you,
At noon today had happened to be killed—
I should not cry aloud—I could not cry
Aloud, or wring my hands in such a place—
I should but watch the station lights rush by
With a more careful interest on my face;
Or raise my eyes and read with greater care
Where to store furs and how to treat the hair.

There are few poems which can equal this one's depiction of the impersonality of the modern city and the emotional vortexes which swirl beneath it.

A Few Figs For Thistles and *Second April* (both 1921) were conceived of by Millay as companion volumes, the first made up of light verse, the second of more weighty poems. However, *Few Figs*, with its sexy, insatiable, insouciant speakers, created such a flurry that it overshadowed the other book, and earned Millay a reputation for flippancy. The critics chided, and asked where the young Romantic of "Renascence" had gone, but her young public loved it and quoted its poems merrily all over New York and Paris: "We were very tired, we were very merry—/ We had gone back and forth all night on the ferry" ("Recuerdo"); "And if I loved you Wednesday, / Well, what is that to you? / I do not love you Thursday—/ So much is true" ("Thursday"); "The fabric of my faithful love / No power shall dim or ravel / Whilst I stay here,—but oh, my dear, / If I should ever travel!" ("To the Not Impossible Him"). Such lines had never been heard from a woman poet before. Here was female sexuality so exuberant and unabashed that it played like innocence. Millay's speakers were women who loved love—"Oh, think not I am faithful to a vow! / Faithless am I save to love's self alone"—and the poems were about their own experience of passion more than about any one man who might afford the occasion for it.

> I shall forget you presently, my dear,
> So make the most of this, your little day,
> Your little month, your little half a year,
> Ere I forget, or die, or move away,
> And we are done forever. . . .

In poems such as this, Millay manhandles the materials of the Renaissance *carpe diem* tradition in order to assert a woman's right to inconstancy and, tongue firmly in cheek, to bemoan the perishable beauties of men. Where earlier sonneteers such as Petrarch, Sidney, Wyatt, and Shakespeare used the opportunity to memorialize their mistress' beauties as a way of asserting the power and permanence of their own poems, Millay escapes from the woman's designated position as object (both sexual and poetic) in order to claim that her own unquenchable passions provide her with an inexhaustible fund of poetic material. Modern love is, she tells us, ephemeral. The desirous self panting for experience is the only constant thing.

Second April, though less popular with the public than *A Few Figs*, garnered much greater critical respect. It contains some of Millay's most effective nature poems, especially those that invoke the Maine landscape of her childhood, such as "Eel-Grass," "Low-Tide," "Exiled" (one of Millay's most musical poems), and "Inland" with its "water sucking the hollow ledges" and its waves "Spanking the boats at the harbor's head." In these poems, Millay's voice resembles that of Robert Frost in its particularity and precision regarding place. Here too are some of her most effective poems about death and the poignancy of time's passing: "Passer Mortuus Est" with its "little petulant hand" becomes "an annotation," and "Elegy Before Death" with its catalog of all the beautiful things that the death of the loved one will not alter, and its wonderfully quiet closing:

> Oh, there will pass with your great passing
>   Little of beauty not your own,
> Only the light from common water,
>   Only the grace from simple stone!

Notable as well is the series "Memorial to D. C." written in memory of Millay's Vassar classmate, Dorothy Coleman, with its combination of classical allusion and homely detail (the dead girl's closet full of unworn shoes, the memory of her "indefinite-coloured hair"). The volume closes with twelve sonnets, among which are some of Millay's finest, such as "Into the golden vessel of great song" and "Not with libations, but with shouts and laughter." These sonnets, unlike the "child poems"—"Renascence," "The Ballad of the Harp-Weaver," "The Bean-Stalk"—speak in a seasoned voice, at once learned and impassioned, whose tonal modulations and formal finesse represent the very best of Millay's style. They demonstrate the emotional depths and rich ironies which could be achieved by the modern woman's appropriation, rather than mere imitation, of a traditionally masculine form.

Millay's involvement with the theater as playwright, director, and actress complemented both the theatrical and historical tendencies of her poetry. Though the plays she wrote as a teenager were set in modern times, the ones she wrote in college and immediately after, three of which are reproduced in this volume, were all verse dramas based on medieval and Renaissance models. *Two Slatterns and a King* (1920), first produced in 1919 by the Provincetown Players, is a light farce modeled on medieval morality plays, in which a king sets out to marry a model housewife. Through the machinations of Chance (the narrator), Tidy, who is usually fastidious, lets her house go to ruins on the day the king visits; Slut, who is typically a slattern, decides to clean up as a novel amusement, and ends up winning the king's hand. Though the explicit moral is that no one can control chance (and, of course, good housekeeping is all about control), the submerged moral seems to be a feminist one: men's attempts to control and reward women's virtue (terms such as "Slut" and "slattern" suggest that sexual virtue is at issue) will inevitably backfire, since women can appear to be what they are not (that there are "two slatterns" suggests that no women are truly "chaste").

The Lamp and the Bell (1921), a quasi-Renaissance pageant commissioned for the fiftieth anniversary of the Vassar College Alumni Association, is, like *Two Slatterns,* a kind of fairy tale. Modeled on "Rose White and Rose Red," it tells the tale of two stepsisters divided by a jealous mother and a disloyal man, who nonetheless remain loyal to one another. Though some commentators dismissed the play as a "lesbian" allegory, its theme of female solidarity—and its enormous cast of courtiers, pages, and soldiers—suited its occasion, and its leavening of Elizabethan atmosphere and wit with modern attitudes showcased Millay's talent for reworking historical modes. Like many women writers both before and after her (Christina Rossetti, Marianne Moore, and Anne Sexton, to name a few), Millay found the fairy tale an apt vehicle, in both plays and poems, for revisiting cultural assumptions about gender, virtue, and power.

Aria da Capo (1920), Millay's most admired play, was the hit of the 1919–1920 season at the Provincetown Playhouse, where it was directed by Millay and starred her sister Norma in the role of Columbine. The play combines elements of commedia dell'arte and theater of the absurd into an effective anti-war allegory. In the play, two lovers, Pierrot and Columbine, exchange silly banter as they dine sumptuously. But when they leave the stage, two shepherds enter and are directed by Cothurnus (a Fate-like figure), to enact their own scene, though the set is not appropriate and they have difficulty remembering their parts. Their scene requires that they play at building a wall between themselves out of paper ribbon; when one discovers jewels on his side of the wall, and the other discovers water, each of which they refuse to share, their game turns earnest and leads to mutual slaughter. When Pierrot and Columbine return to discover the bodies, and object that they cannot continue their part of the play with dead bodies onstage, Cothurnus urges them to shove the bodies under the table, reassuring them that "the audience will forget." The play's title, which refers to a musical direction to repeat, suggests that the trivialities of everyday social life, and the senseless eruptions of greed and violence being enacted alongside them, will continue their cycle without end as long as the witnesses to history are willing to forget. While the petty misunderstandings of the lovers seem to be a distraction from the tragic conflict between the shepherds, the play's placing of them together on the same set suggests that the daily battles between men and women may be more than incidentally related to the impulses which lead to war, an idea which prefigures the argument made by Virginia Woolf in her feminist anti-war manifesto, *Three Guineas*.

Though Millay is one of the most beloved—and most often memorized—of modern poets, the critical assessments of Millay's work have never equaled the passionate admiration of her fans. There are a number of reasons for this. First, in an era in which many poets were experimenting with innovative forms and throwing off rhyme and meter, Millay continued to employ the themes and structures of earlier Renaissance and Romantic verse. While this practice rendered her poetry recognizably "poetic" to a general audience, it led many avant-garde writers and critics to conclude that her work was merely derivative or old-fashioned, a remnant of the conventional literary practices which modernism was attempting to overthrow. Second, at a time when poems such as T. S. Eliot's "The Waste Land" or Ezra Pound's "Hugh Selwyn Mauberly" were depicting the modern subject as alienated or nihilistic and attempting to distance poetry from its source in the poet's private feelings, Millay spoke directly to the topic of love—heterosexual, homoerotic, platonic, and communal—in poems which foregrounded the personal and the emotional. Third, as many poets of the early twentieth century moved away from explicit engagement with social and political questions, towards poetry as a purely aesthetic realm, Millay persisted in using both her poetry and her plays to address questions of war, injustice, and gender inequality. And, finally, while many modernists were cultivating an elite coterie of readers through increasingly difficult styles, Millay wrote universally accessible and wildly popular poems which many readers perceived to be speaking directly to and of their own experiences (in the midst of the Depression, *Wine From These Grapes* sold over 66,000 copies in seven months). For all of these reasons, literary historians have found it difficult to place Millay as a modernist poet, often seeing her instead as a holdover from earlier Romantic or sentimental poetic modes or as a precursor of late twentieth-century popular culture with its marketing of "personalities."

As with any celebrity artist, the fascination of Millay's private life (her famous bohemianism, her sexual allure) has been difficult to disentangle from the value of her works and their cultural significance. This is a potential trap for any lyric poet, given that lyric is the literary genre most dependent upon the illusion of a speaking voice and a personal presence. But it is has proved a particularly vexing problem for women poets, who are too often considered first as women, subject to society's expectations regarding womanly attributes and behavior, and only secondarily as poets. Millay's life excited interest in her poems, and often competed with them for attention. But the sense that the poems give unmediated access to the poet's life has tended to diminish readers' appreciation for Millay's erudition and superb craftsmanship, the imaginative range of her works, and the extent to which the conventions of various literary forms such as the ballad, the sonnet, and the elegy help to determine the kinds of identities the speakers of her poems can effectively adopt. Moreover, the emphasis on Millay's poems as merely personal effusions has long obscured the fascinating ways in which these poems both shaped and were shaped by early twentieth-century cultural attitudes about poetic authority, women, sentiment, and sex.

However, in recent decades, the increasing prominence of women writers has generated a desire to re-examine the achievements of literary precursors such as Millay. In addition, feminist approaches to literature have enabled new ways of thinking about women artists' conflicted relationships to the decidedly masculine rhetoric of modernism, and have helped to broaden our sense of the variety of poetic practices in play in the early twentieth century. We now realize that there was more than one way of "making it new." Where early critics often devalued Millay's poems as too "feminine," contemporary critics find both historical and aesthetic value in the feminine (and feminist) perspectives which they bring to questions of sexuality, power, and poetic inheritance. Perhaps most significant for a revaluing of Millay, her performability (the theatrical readings, the borrowed forms, the role-playing as Helen or Isolde) may no longer strike readers as insincere, but rather as the very embodiment of the postmodern self. Madonna may, oddly enough, have given us back Millay.

Stacy Carson Hubbard is Associate Professor of English at the State University of New York at Buffalo. She has published essays on Edna St. Vincent Millay, Marianne Moore, Gwendolyn Brooks and other modern women poets, and is currently working on a project concerning questions of sympathy and self-reliance in American women's writing.

❧ PART I ❧

SELECTED POETRY OF
EDNA ST. VINCENT MILLAY

Renascence and other Poems

RENASCENCE AND OTHER POEMS

Renascence

All I could see from where I stood
Was three long mountains and a wood;
I turned and looked another way,
And saw three islands in a bay.
So with my eyes I traced the line
Of the horizon, thin and fine,
Straight around till I was come
Back to where I'd started from;
And all I saw from where I stood
Was three long mountains and a wood.

Over these things I could not see;
These were the things that bounded me;
And I could touch them with my hand,
Almost, I thought, from where I stand.
And all at once things seemed so small
My breath came short, and scarce at all.
But, sure, the sky is big, I said;
Miles and miles above my head;
So here upon my back I'll lie
And look my fill into the sky.
And so I looked, and, after all,

The sky was not so very tall.
The sky, I said, must somewhere stop,
And—sure enough!—I see the top!
The sky, I thought, is not so grand;
I 'most could touch it with my hand!
And reaching up my hand to try,
I screamed to feel it touch the sky.

I screamed, and—lo!—Infinity
Came down and settled over me;
Forced back my scream into my chest,
Bent back my arm upon my breast,
And, pressing of the Undefined
The definition on my mind,
Held up before my eyes a glass
Through which my shrinking sight did pass
Until it seemed I must behold
Immensity made manifold;
Whispered to me a word whose sound
Deafened the air for worlds around,
And brought unmuffled to my ears
The gossiping of friendly spheres,
The creaking of the tented sky,
The ticking of Eternity.

I saw and heard, and knew at last
The How and Why of all things, past,
And present, and forevermore.
The Universe, cleft to the core,
Lay open to my probing sense
That, sick'ning, I would fain pluck thence
But could not,—nay! But needs must suck
At the great wound, and could not pluck
My lips away till I had drawn
All venom out.—Ah, fearful pawn!
For my omniscience paid I toll

In infinite remorse of soul.
All sin was of my sinning, all
Atoning mine, and mine the gall
Of all regret. Mine was the weight
Of every brooded wrong, the hate
That stood behind each envious thrust,
Mine every greed, mine every lust.

And all the while for every grief,
Each suffering, I craved relief
With individual desire,—
Craved all in vain! And felt fierce fire
About a thousand people crawl;
Perished with each,—then mourned for all!
A man was starving in Capri;
He moved his eyes and looked at me;
I felt his gaze, I heard his moan,
And knew his hunger as my own.

I saw at sea a great fog bank
Between two ships that struck and sank;
A thousand screams the heavens smote;
And every scream tore through my throat.

No hurt I did not feel, no death
That was not mine; mine each last breath
That, crying, met an answering cry
From the compassion that was I.
All suffering mine, and mine its rod;
Mine, pity like the pity of God.

Ah, awful weight! Infinity
Pressed down upon the finite Me!
My anguished spirit, like a bird,
Beating against my lips I heard;
Yet lay the weight so close about

There was no room for it without.
And so beneath the weight lay I
And suffered death, but could not die.

Long had I lain thus, craving death,
When quietly the earth beneath
Gave way, and inch by inch, so great
At last had grown the crushing weight,
Into the earth I sank till I
Full six feet under ground did lie,
And sank no more,—there is no weight
Can follow here, however great.
From off my breast I felt it roll,
And as it went my tortured soul
Burst forth and fled in such a gust
That all about me swirled the dust.
Deep in the earth I rested now;
Cool is its hand upon the brow
And soft its breast beneath the head
Of one who is so gladly dead.
And all at once, and over all
The pitying rain began to fall;
I lay and heard each pattering hoof
Upon my lowly, thatched roof,
And seemed to love the sound far more
Than ever I had done before.
For rain it hath a friendly sound
To one who's six feet underground;
And scarce the friendly voice or face:
A grave is such a quiet place.

The rain, I said, is kind to come
And speak to me in my new home.
I would I were alive again
To kiss the fingers of the rain,

To drink into my eyes the shine
Of every slanting silver line,
To catch the freshened, fragrant breeze
From drenched and dripping apple-trees.
For soon the shower will be done,
And then the broad face of the sun
Will laugh above the rain-soaked earth
Until the world with answering mirth
Shakes joyously, and each round drop
Rolls, twinkling, from its grass-blade top.

How can I bear it; buried here,
While overhead the sky grows clear
And blue again after the storm?
O, multi-colored, multiform,
Beloved beauty over me,
That I shall never, never see
Again! Spring-silver, autumn-gold,
That I shall never more behold!
Sleeping your myriad magics through,
Close-sepulchred away from you!
O God, I cried, give me new birth,
And put me back upon the earth!
Upset each cloud's gigantic gourd
And let the heavy rain, down-poured
In one big torrent, set me free,
Washing my grave away from me!

I ceased; and through the breathless hush
That answered me, the far-off rush
Of herald wings came whispering
Like music down the vibrant string
Of my ascending prayer, and—crash!
Before the wild wind's whistling lash
The startled storm-clouds reared on high

And plunged in terror down the sky,
And the big rain in one black wave
Fell from the sky and struck my grave.

I know not how such things can be;
I only know there came to me
A fragrance such as never clings
To aught save happy living things;
A sound as of some joyous elf
Singing sweet songs to please himself,
And, through and over everything,
A sense of glad awakening.
The grass, a-tiptoe at my ear,
Whispering to me I could hear;
I felt the rain's cool finger-tips
Brushed tenderly across my lips,
Laid gently on my sealed sight,
And all at once the heavy night
Fell from my eyes and I could see,—
A drenched and dripping apple-tree,
A last long line of silver rain,
A sky grown clear and blue again.
And as I looked a quickening gust
Of wind blew up to me and thrust
Into my face a miracle
Of orchard-breath, and with the smell,—
I know not how such things can be!—
I breathed my soul back into me.

Ah! Up then from the ground sprang I
And hailed the earth with such a cry
As is not heard save from a man
Who has been dead, and lives again.
About the trees my arms I wound;
Like one gone mad I hugged the ground;
I raised my quivering arms on high;

I laughed and laughed into the sky,
Till at my throat a strangling sob
Caught fiercely, and a great heart-throb
Sent instant tears into my eyes;
O God, I cried, no dark disguise
Can e'er hereafter hide from me
Thy radiant identity!
Thou canst not move across the grass
But my quick eyes will see Thee pass,
Nor speak, however silently,
But my hushed voice will answer Thee.
I know the path that tells Thy way
Through the cool eve of everyday;
God, I can push the grass apart
And lay my finger on Thy heart!

The world stands out on either side
No wider than the heart is wide;
Above the world is stretched the sky,—
No higher than the soul is high.
The heart can push the sea and land
Farther away on either hand;
The soul can split the sky in two,
And let the face of God shine through.
But East and West will pinch the heart
That can not keep them pushed apart;
And he whose soul is flat—the sky
Will cave in on him by and by.

Interim

The room is full of you!—As I came in
And closed the door behind me, all at once
A something in the air, intangible,
Yet stiff with meaning, struck my senses sick!—
Sharp, unfamiliar odors have destroyed

Each other room's dear personality.
The heavy scent of damp, funereal flowers,—
The very essence, hush-distilled, of Death—
Has strangled that habitual breath of home
Whose expiration leaves all houses dead;
And wheresoe'er I look is hideous change.
Save here. Here 'twas as if a weed-choked gate
Had opened at my touch, and I had stepped
Into some long-forgot, enchanted, strange,
Sweet garden of a thousand years ago
And suddenly thought, "I have been here before!"

You are not here. I know that you are gone,
And will not ever enter here again.
And yet it seems to me, if I should speak,
Your silent step must wake across the hall;
If I should turn my head, that your sweet eyes
Would kiss me from the door.—So short a time
To teach my life its transposition to
This difficult and unaccustomed key!—
The room is as you left it; your last touch—
A thoughtless pressure, knowing not itself
As saintly—hallows now each simple thing;
Hallows and glorifies, and glows between
The dust's grey fingers like a shielded light.

There is your book, just as you laid it down,
Face to the table,—I cannot believe
That you are gone!—Just then it seemed to me
You must be here. I almost laughed to think
How like reality the dream had been;
Yet knew before I laughed, and so was still.
That book, outspread, just as you laid it down!
Perhaps you thought, "I wonder what comes next,
And whether this or this will be the end";
So rose, and left it, thinking to return.

Perhaps that chair, when you arose and passed
Out of the room, rocked silently a while
Ere it again was still. When you were gone
Forever from the room, perhaps that chair,
Stirred by your movement, rocked a little while,
Silently, to and fro . . .

And here are the last words your fingers wrote,
Scrawled in broad characters across a page
In this brown book I gave you. Here your hand,
Guiding your rapid pen, moved up and down.
Here with a looping knot you crossed a "t",
And here another like it, just beyond
These two eccentric "e's." You were so small,
And wrote so brave a hand!
                              How strange it seems
That of all words these are the words you chose!
And yet a simple choice; you did not know
You would not write again. If you had known—
But then, it does not matter,—and indeed
If you had known there was so little time
You would have dropped your pen and come to me
And this page would be empty, and some phrase
Other than this would hold my wonder now.
Yet, since you could not know, and it befell
That these are the last words your fingers wrote,
There is a dignity some might not see
In this, "I picked the first sweet-pea today."
Today! Was there an opening bud beside it
You left until tomorrow?—O my love,
The things that withered,—and you came not back!
That day you filled this circle of my arms
That now is empty. (O my empty life!)
That day—that day you picked the first sweet-pea,—
And brought it in to show me! I recall
With terrible distinctness how the smell

Of your cool gardens drifted in with you.
I know, you held it up for me to see
And flushed because I looked not at the flower,
But at your face; and when behind my look
You saw such unmistakable intent
You laughed and brushed your flower against my lips.
(You were the fairest thing God ever made,
I think.) And then your hands above my heart
Drew down its stem into a fastening,
And while your head was bent I kissed your hair.
I wonder if you knew. (Beloved hands!
Somehow I cannot seem to see them still.
Somehow I cannot seem to see the dust
In your bright hair.) What is the need of Heaven
When earth can be so sweet?—If only God
Had let us love,—and show the world the way!
Strange cancellings must ink th' eternal books
When love-crossed-out will bring the answer right!

That first sweet-pea! I wonder where it is.
It seems to me I laid it down somewhere,
And yet,—I am not sure. I am not sure,
Even, if it was white or pink; for then
'Twas much like any other flower to me,
Save that it was the first. I did not know,
Then, that it was the last. If I had known—
But then, it does not matter. Strange how few,
After all's said and done, the things that are
Of moment.
            Few indeed! When I can make
Of ten small words a rope to hang the world!
"I had you and I have you now no more."
There, there it dangles,—where's the little truth
That can for long keep footing under that
When its slack syllables tighten to a thought?
Here, let me write it down! I wish to see
Just how a thing like that will look on paper!

"I had you and I have you now no more."

O little words, how can you run so straight
Across the page, beneath the weight you bear?
How can you fall apart, whom such a theme
Has bound together, and hereafter aid
In trivial expression, that have been
So hideously dignified?—Would God
That tearing you apart would tear the thread
I strung you on! Would God—O God, my mind
Stretches asunder on this merciless rack
Of imagery! O, let me sleep a while!
Would I could sleep, and wake to find me back
In that sweet summer afternoon with you.
Summer? 'Tis summer still by the calendar!
How easily could God, if He so willed,
Set back the world a little turn or two!
Correct its griefs, and bring its joys again!

We were so wholly one I had not thought
That we could die apart. I had not thought
That I could move,—and you be stiff and still!
That I could speak,—and you perforce be dumb!
I think our heart-strings were, like warp and woof
In some firm fabric, woven in and out;
Your golden filaments in fair design
Across my duller fibre. And today
The shining strip is rent; the exquisite
Fine pattern is destroyed; part of your heart
Aches in my breast; part of my heart lies chilled
In the damp earth with you. I have been torn
In two, and suffer for the rest of me.
What is my life to me? And what am I
To life,—a ship whose star has guttered out?
A Fear that in the deep night starts awake
Perpetually, to find its senses strained

Against the taut strings of the quivering air,
Awaiting the return of some dread chord?
Dark, Dark, is all I find for metaphor;
All else were contrast,—save that contrast's wall
Is down, and all opposed things flow together
Into a vast monotony, where night
And day, and frost and thaw, and death and life,
Are synonyms. What now—what now to me
Are all the jabbering birds and foolish flowers
That clutter up the world? You were my song!
Now, let discord scream! You were my flower!
Now let the world grow weeds! For I shall not
Plant things above your grave—(the common balm
Of the conventional woe for its own wound!)
Amid sensations rendered negative
By your elimination stands today,
Certain, unmixed, the element of grief;
I sorrow; and I shall not mock my truth
With travesties of suffering, nor seek
To effigy its incorporeal bulk
In little wry-faced images of woe.

I cannot call you back; and I desire
No utterance of my immaterial voice.
I cannot even turn my face this way
Or that, and say, "My face is turned to you";
I know not where you are, I do not know
If Heaven hold you or if earth transmute,
Body and soul, you into earth again;
But this I know:—not for one second's space
Shall I insult my sight with visionings
Such as the credulous crowd so eager-eyed
Beholds, self-conjured, in the empty air.
Let the world wail! Let drip its easy tears!
My sorrow shall be dumb!

                    —What do I say?
God! God!—God pity me! Am I gone mad
That I should spit upon a rosary?
Am I become so shrunken? Would to God
I too might feel that frenzied faith whose touch
Makes temporal the most enduring grief;
Though it must walk a while, as is its wont,
With wild lamenting! Would I too might weep
Where weeps the world and hangs its piteous wreaths
For its new dead! Not Truth, but Faith, it is
That keeps the world alive. If all at once
Faith were to slacken,—that unconscious faith
Which must, I know, yet be the corner-stone
Of all believing,—birds now flying fearless
Across would drop in terror to the earth;
Fishes would drown; and the all-governing reins
Would tangle in the frantic hands of God
And the worlds gallop headlong to destruction!

O God, I see it now, and my sick brain
Staggers and swoons! How often over me
Flashes this breathlessness of sudden sight
In which I see the universe unrolled
Before me like a scroll and read thereon
Chaos and Doom, where helpless planets whirl
Dizzily round and round and round and round,
Like tops across a table, gathering speed
With every spin, to waver on the edge
One instant—looking over—and the next
To shudder and lurch forward out of sight—
            *   *   *   *   *
Ah, I am worn out—I am wearied out—
It is too much—I am but flesh and blood,
And I must sleep. Though you were dead again,
I am but flesh and blood and I must sleep.

The Suicide

"Curse thee, Life, I will live with thee no more!
Thou hast mocked me, starved me, beat my body sore!
And all for a pledge that was not pledged by me,
I have kissed thy crust and eaten sparingly
That I might eat again, and met thy sneers
With deprecations, and thy blows with tears,—
Aye, from thy glutted lash, glad, crawled away,
As if spent passion were a holiday!
And now I go. Nor threat, nor easy vow
Of tardy kindness can avail thee now
With me, whence fear and faith alike are flown;
Lonely I came, and I depart alone,
And know not where nor unto whom I go;
But that thou canst not follow me I know."

Thus I to Life, and ceased; but through my brain
My thought ran still, until I spake again:

"Ah, but I go not as I came,—no trace
Is mine to bear away of that old grace
I brought! I have been heated in thy fires,
Bent by thy hands, fashioned to thy desires,
Thy mark is on me! I am not the same
Nor ever more shall be, as when I came.
Ashes am I of all that once I seemed.
In me all's sunk that leapt, and all that dreamed
Is wakeful for alarm,—oh, shame to thee,
For the ill change that thou hast wrought in me,
Who laugh no more nor lift my throat to sing!
Ah, Life, I would have been a pleasant thing
To have about the house when I was grown
If thou hadst left my little joys alone!
I asked of thee no favor save this one:

That thou wouldst leave me playing in the sun!
And this thou didst deny, calling my name
Insistently, until I rose and came.
I saw the sun no more.—It were not well
So long on these unpleasant thoughts to dwell,
Need I arise tomorrow and renew
Again my hated tasks, but I am through
With all things save my thoughts and this one night,
So that in truth I seem already quite
Free and remote from thee,—I feel no haste
And no reluctance to depart; I taste
Merely, with thoughtful mien, an unknown draught,
That in a little while I shall have quaffed."
Thus I to Life, and ceased, and slightly smiled,
Looking at nothing; and my thin dreams filed
Before me one by one till once again
I set new words unto an old refrain:

"Treasures thou hast that never have been mine!
Warm lights in many a secret chamber shine
Of thy gaunt house, and gusts of song have blown
Like blossoms out to me that sat alone!
And I have waited well for thee to show
If any share were mine,—and now I go!
Nothing I leave, and if I naught attain
I shall but come into mine own again!"
Thus I to Life, and ceased, and spake no more,
But turning, straightway, sought a certain door
In the rear wall. Heavy it was, and low
And dark,—a way by which none e'er would go
That other exit had, and never knock
Was heard thereat,—bearing a curious lock
Some chance had shown me fashioned faultily,
Whereof Life held content the useless key,
And great coarse hinges, thick and rough with rust,
Whose sudden voice across a silence must,

I knew, be harsh and horrible to hear,—
A strange door, ugly like a dwarf.—So near
I came I felt upon my feet the chill
Of acid wind creeping across the sill.
So stood longtime, till over me at last
Came weariness, and all things other passed
To make it room; the still night drifted deep
Like snow about me, and I longed for sleep.

But, suddenly, marking the morning hour,
Bayed the deep-throated bell within the tower!
Startled, I raised my head,—and with a shout
Laid hold upon the latch,—and was without.

    *   *   *   *   *

Ah, long-forgotten, well-remembered road,
Leading me back unto my old abode,
My father's house! There in the night I came,
And found them feasting, and all things the same
As they had been before. A splendour hung
Upon the walls, and such sweet songs were sung
As, echoing out of very long ago,
Had called me from the house of Life, I know.
So fair their raiment shone I looked in shame
On the unlovely garb in which I came;
Then straightway at my hesitancy mocked:
"It is my father's house!" I said and knocked;
And the door opened. To the shining crowd
Tattered and dark I entered, like a cloud,
Seeing no face but his; to him I crept,
And "Father!" I cried, and clasped his knees, and wept.
Ah, days of joy that followed! All alone
I wandered through the house. My own, my own,
My own to touch, my own to taste and smell,
All I had lacked so long and loved so well!
None shook me out of sleep, nor hushed my song,
Nor called me in from the sunlight all day long.

I know not when the wonder came to me
Of what my father's business might be,
And whither fared and on what errands bent
The tall and gracious messengers he sent.
Yet one day with no song from dawn till night
Wondering, I sat, and watched them out of sight.
And the next day I called; and on the third
Asked them if I might go,—but no one heard.
Then, sick with longing, I arose at last
And went unto my father,—in that vast
Chamber wherein he for so many years
Has sat, surrounded by his charts and spheres.
"Father," I said, "Father, I cannot play
The harp that thou didst give me, and all day
I sit in idleness, while to and fro
About me thy serene, grave servants go;
And I am weary of my lonely ease.
Better a perilous journey overseas
Away from thee, than this, the life I lead,
To sit all day in the sunshine like a weed
That grows to naught,—I love thee more than they
Who serve thee most; yet serve thee in no way.
Father, I beg of thee a little task
To dignify my days,—'tis all I ask
Forever, but forever, this denied,
I perish."

      "Child," my father's voice replied,
"All things thy fancy hath desired of me
Thou hast received. I have prepared for thee
Within my house a spacious chamber, where
Are delicate things to handle and to wear,
And all these things are thine. Dost thou love song?
My minstrels shall attend thee all day long.
Or sigh for flowers? My fairest gardens stand
Open as fields to thee on every hand.
And all thy days this word shall hold the same:

No pleasure shalt thou lack that thou shalt name.
But as for tasks—" he smiled, and shook his head;
"Thou hadst thy task, and laidst it by," he said.

God's World

O world, I cannot hold thee close enough!
　　Thy winds, thy wide grey skies!
　　Thy mists, that roll and rise!
Thy woods, this autumn day, that ache and sag
And all but cry with colour! That gaunt crag
To crush! To lift the lean of that black bluff!
World, World, I cannot get thee close enough!

Long have I known a glory in it all,
　　　　But never knew I this;
　　　　Here such a passion is
As stretcheth me apart,—Lord, I do fear
Thou'st made the world too beautiful this year;
My soul is all but out of me,—let fall
No burning leaf; prithee, let no bird call.

Afternoon on a Hill

I will be the gladdest thing
　　Under the sun!
I will touch a hundred flowers
　　And not pick one.

I will look at cliffs and clouds
　　With quiet eyes,
Watch the wind bow down the grass,
　　And the grass rise.

And when lights begin to show
    Up from the town,
I will mark which must be mine,
    And then start down!

Sorrow

Sorrow like a ceaseless rain
    Beats upon my heart.
People twist and scream in pain,—
Dawn will find them still again;
This has neither wax nor wane,
    Neither stop nor start.

People dress and go to town;
    I sit in my chair.
All my thoughts are slow and brown:
Standing up or sitting down
Little matters, or what gown
    Or what shoes I wear.

Tavern

I'll keep a little tavern
    Below the high hill's crest,
Wherein all grey-eyed people
    May set them down and rest.

There shall be plates a-plenty,
    And mugs to melt the chill
Of all the grey-eyed people
    Who happen up the hill.

There sound will sleep the traveller,
 And dream his journey's end,
But I will rouse at midnight
 The falling fire to tend.

Aye, 'tis a curious fancy—
 But all the good I know
Was taught me out of two grey eyes
 A long time ago.

Ashes of Life

Love has gone and left me and the days are all alike;
 Eat I must, and sleep I will,—and would that night were here!
But ah!—to lie awake and hear the slow hours strike!
 Would that it were day again!—with twilight near!

Love has gone and left me and I don't know what to do;
 This or that or what you will is all the same to me;
But all the things that I begin I leave before I'm through,—
 There's little use in anything as far as I can see.

Love has gone and left me,—and the neighbors knock and borrow,
 And life goes on forever like the gnawing of a mouse,—
And tomorrow and tomorrow and tomorrow and tomorrow
 There's this little street and this little house.

The Little Ghost

I knew her for a little ghost
 That in my garden walked;
The wall is high—higher than most—
 And the green gate was locked.

And yet I did not think of that
    Till after she was gone—
I knew her by the broad white hat,
    All ruffled, she had on.

By the dear ruffles round her feet,
    By her small hands that hung
In their lace mitts, austere and sweet,
    Her gown's white folds among.

I watched to see if she would stay,
    What she would do—and oh!
She looked as if she liked the way
    I let my garden grow!

She bent above my favourite mint
    With conscious garden grace,
She smiled and smiled—there was no hint
    Of sadness in her face.

She held her gown on either side
    To let her slippers show,
And up the walk she went with pride,
    The way great ladies go.

And where the wall is built in new
    And is of ivy bare
She paused—then opened and passed through
    A gate that once was there.

Kin to Sorrow

Am I kin to Sorrow,
    That so oft
Falls the knocker of my door—
    Neither loud nor soft,

But as long accustomed,
    Under Sorrow's hand?
Marigolds around the step
    And rosemary stand,
And then comes Sorrow—
    And what does Sorrow care
For the rosemary
    Or the marigolds there?
Am I kin to Sorrow?
    Are we kin?
That so oft upon my door—
    Oh, come in!

Three Songs of Shattering

I

The first rose on my rose-tree
    Budded, bloomed, and shattered,
During sad days when to me
    Nothing mattered.

Grief of grief has drained me clean;
    Still it seems a pity
No one saw,—it must have been
    Very pretty.

II

Let the little birds sing;
    Let the little lambs play;
Spring is here; and so 'tis spring;—
    But not in the old way!

I recall a place
    Where a plum-tree grew;
There you lifted up your face,
    And blossoms covered you.

If the little birds sing,
    And the little lambs play,
Spring is here; and so 'tis spring—
    But not in the old way!

III

All the dog-wood blossoms are underneath the tree!
    Ere spring was going—ah, spring is gone!
And there comes no summer to the like of you and me,—
    Blossom time is early, but no fruit sets on.

All the dog-wood blossoms are underneath the tree,
    Browned at the edges, turned in a day;
And I would with all my heart they trimmed a mound for me,
    And weeds were tall on all the paths that led that way!

The Shroud

Death, I say, my heart is bowed
    Unto thine,—O mother!
This red gown will make a shroud
    Good as any other!

(I, that would not wait to wear
    My own bridal things,
In a dress dark as my hair
    Made my answerings.

I, tonight, that till he came
    Could not, could not wait,
In a gown as bright as flame
    Held for them the gate.)

Death, I say, my heart is bowed
    Unto thine,—O mother!
This red gown will make a shroud
    Good as any other!

The Dream

Love, if I weep it will not matter,
    And if you laugh I shall not care;
Foolish am I to think about it,
    But it is good to feel you there.

Love, in my sleep I dreamed of waking,—
    White and awful the moonlight reached
Over the floor, and somewhere, somewhere,
    There was a shutter loose,—it screeched!

Swung in the wind,—and no wind blowing!—
    I was afraid, and turned to you,
Put out my hand to you for comfort,—
    And you were gone! Cold, cold as dew,

Under my hand the moonlight lay!
    Love, if you laugh I shall not care,
But if I weep it will not matter,—
    Ah, it is good to feel you there!

Indifference

I said,—for Love was laggard, O, Love was slow to come,—
    "I'll hear his step and know his step when I am warm in bed;
But I'll never leave my pillow, though there be some
    As would let him in—and take him in with tears!" I said.
I lay,—for Love was laggard, O, he came not until dawn,—
    I lay and listened for his step and could not get to sleep;
And he found me at my window with my big cloak on,
    All sorry with the tears some folks might weep!

Witch-Wife

She is neither pink nor pale,
     And she never will be all mine;
She learned her hands in a fairy-tale,
     And her mouth on a valentine.

She has more hair than she needs;
     In the sun 'tis a woe to me!
And her voice is a string of colored beads,
Or steps leading into the sea.
She loves me all that she can,
     And her ways to my ways resign;
But she was not made for any man,
     And she never will be all mine.

Blight

Hard seeds of hate I planted
     That should by now be grown,—
Rough stalks, and from thick stamens
     A poisonous pollen blown,
And odors rank, unbreathable,
     From dark corollas thrown!

At dawn from my damp garden
     I shook the chilly dew;
The thin boughs locked behind me
     That sprang to let me through;
The blossoms slept,—I sought a place
     Where nothing lovely grew.

And there, when day was breaking,
  I knelt and looked around:
The light was near, the silence
  Was palpitant with sound;
I drew my hate from out my breast
  And thrust it in the ground.

Oh, ye so fiercely tended,
  Ye little seeds of hate!
I bent above your growing
  Early and noon and late,
Yet are ye drooped and pitiful,—
  I cannot rear ye straight!

The sun seeks out my garden,
  No nook is left in shade,
No mist nor mold nor mildew
  Endures on any blade,
Sweet rain slants under every bough:
  Ye falter, and ye fade.

When the Year Grows Old

I cannot but remember
  When the year grows old—
October—November—
  How she disliked the cold!

She used to watch the swallows
  Go down across the sky,
And turn from the window
  With a little sharp sigh.

And often when the brown leaves
  Were brittle on the ground,
And the wind in the chimney
  Made a melancholy sound,

She had a look about her
    That I wish I could forget—
The look of a scared thing
    Sitting in a net!

Oh, beautiful at nightfall
    The soft spitting snow!
And beautiful the bare boughs
    Rubbing to and fro!

But the roaring of the fire,
    And the warmth of fur,
And the boiling of the kettle
    Were beautiful to her!

I cannot but remember
    When the year grows old—
October—November—
    How she disliked the cold!

Sonnets

I

Thou art not lovelier than lilacs,—no,
    Nor honeysuckle; thou art not more fair
    Than small white single poppies,—I can bear
Thy beauty; though I bend before thee, though
From left to right, not knowing where to go,
    I turn my troubled eyes, nor here nor there
    Find any refuge from thee, yet I swear
So has it been with mist,—with moonlight so.

Like him who day by day unto his draught
    Of delicate poison adds him one drop more
Till he may drink unharmed the death often,

Even so, inured to beauty, who have quaffed
    Each hour more deeply than the hour before,
I drink—and live—what has destroyed some men.

II

Time does not bring relief; you all have lied
    Who told me time would ease me of my pain!
    I miss him in the weeping of the rain;
I want him at the shrinking of the tide;
The old snows melt from every mountain-side,
    And last year's leaves are smoke in every lane;
    But last year's bitter loving must remain
Heaped on my heart, and my old thoughts abide!

There are a hundred places where I fear
    To go,—so with his memory they brim!
And entering with relief some quiet place
Where never fell his foot or shone his face
I say, "There is no memory of him here!"
    And so stand stricken, so remembering him!

III

Mindful of you the sodden earth in spring,
    And all the flowers that in the springtime grow,
    And dusty roads, and thistles, and the slow
Rising of the round moon, all throats that sing
The summer through, and each departing wing,
    And all the nests that the bared branches show,
    And all winds that in any weather blow,
And all the storms that the four seasons bring.

You go no more on your exultant feet
    Up paths that only mist and morning knew,
Or watch the wind, or listen to the beat

Of a bird's wings too high in air to view,—
But you were something more than young and sweet
And fair,—and the long year remembers you.

IV

Not in this chamber only at my birth—
When the long hours of that mysterious night
Were over, and the morning was in sight—
I cried, but in strange places, steppe and firth
I have not seen, through alien grief and mirth;
And never shall one room contain me quite
Who in so many rooms first saw the light,
Child of all mothers, native of the earth.

So is no warmth for me at any fire
Today, when the world's fire has burned so low;
I kneel, spending my breath in vain desire,
At that cold hearth which one time roared so strong,
And straighten back in weariness, and long
To gather up my little gods and go.

V

If I should learn, in some quite casual way,
That you were gone, not to return again—
Read from the back-page of a paper, say,
Held by a neighbor in a subway train,
How at the corner of this avenue
And such a street (so are the papers filled)
A hurrying man—who happened to be you—
At noon today had happened to be killed,
I should not cry aloud—I could not cry
Aloud, or wring my hands in such a place—

I should but watch the station lights rush by
    With a more careful interest on my face,
Or raise my eyes and read with greater care
Where to store furs and how to treat the hair.

VI

Bluebeard

This door you might not open, and you did;
    So enter now, and see for what slight thing
You are betrayed. . . . Here is no treasure hid,
    No cauldron, no clear crystal mirroring
The sought-for truth, no heads of women slain
    For greed like yours, no writhings of distress,
But only what you see. . . . Look yet again—
    An empty room, cobwebbed and comfortless.
Yet this alone out of my life I kept
    Unto myself, lest any know me quite;
And you did so profane me when you crept
    Unto the threshold of this room tonight
That I must never more behold your face.
    This now is yours. I seek another place.

A Few Figs from Thistles

A Few Figs from Thistles

First Fig

My candle burns at both ends;
 It will not last the night;
But ah, my foes, and oh, my friends—
 It gives a lovely light!

Second Fig

Safe upon the solid rock the ugly houses stand:
 Come and see my shining palace built upon the sand!

Recuerdo

We were very tired, we were very merry—
We had gone back and forth all night on the ferry.
It was bare and bright, and smelled like a stable—
But we looked into a fire, we leaned across a table,
We lay on a hill-top underneath the moon;
And the whistles kept blowing, and the dawn came soon.

We were very tired, we were very merry—
We had gone back and forth all night on the ferry;
And you ate an apple, and I ate a pear,
From a dozen of each we had bought somewhere;
And the sky went wan, and the wind came cold,
And the sun rose dripping, a bucketful of gold.

We were very tired, we were very merry,
We had gone back and forth all night on the ferry.
We hailed, "Good morrow, mother!" to a shawl-covered head,

And bought a morning paper, which neither of us read;
And she wept, "God bless you!" for the apples and pears,
And we gave her all our money but our subway fares.

Thursday

And if I loved you Wednesday,
        Well, what is that to you?
I do not love you Thursday—
        So much is true.

And why you come complaining
        Is more than I can see.
I loved you Wednesday,—yes—but what
        Is that to me?

To the Not Impossible Him

How shall I know, unless I go
        To Cairo and Cathay,
Whether or not this blessed spot
        Is blest in every way?

Now it may be, the flower for me
    Is this beneath my nose;
How shall I tell, unless I smell
    The Carthaginian rose?

The fabric of my faithful love
    No power shall dim or ravel
Whilst I stay here,—but oh, my dear
    If I should ever travel!

Macdougal Street

As I went walking up and down to take the evening air,
    (Sweet to meet upon the street, why must I be so shy?)
I saw him lay his hand upon her torn black hair;
    ("Little dirty Latin child, let the lady by!")

The women squatting on the stoops were slovenly and fat,
    (Lay me out in organdie, lay me out in lawn!)
And everywhere I stepped there was a baby or a cat;
    (Lord, God in Heaven, will it never be dawn?)

The fruit-carts and clam-carts were ribald as a fair,
    (Pink nets and wet shells trodden under heel)
She had haggled from the fruit-man of his rotting ware;
    (I shall never get to sleep, the way I feel!)

He walked like a king through the filth and the clutter,
    (Sweet to meet upon the street, why did you glance me by?)

But he caught the quaint Italian quip she flung him from the gutter;
    (What can there be to cry about that I should lie and cry?)

He laid his darling hand upon her little black head,
    (I wish I were a ragged child with ear-rings in my ears!)
And he said she was a baggage to have said what she had said;
    (Truly I shall be ill unless I stop these tears!)

The Singing-Woman from the Wood's Edge

What should I be but a prophet and a liar,
Whose mother was a leprechaun, whose father was a friar?
Teethed on a crucifix and cradled under water,
What should I be but the fiend's god-daughter?

And who should be my playmates but the adder and the frog,
That was got beneath a furze-bush and born in a bog?
And what should be my singing, that was christened at an altar,
But Aves and Credos and Psalms out of the Psalter?

You will see such webs on the wet grass, maybe,
As a pixie-mother weaves for her baby,
You will find such flame at the wave's weedy ebb
As flashes in the meshes of a mer-mother's web,

But there comes to birth no common spawn
From the love of a priest for a leprechaun,
And you never have seen and you never will see
Such things as the things that swaddled me!

After all's said and after all's done,
What should I be but a harlot and a nun?

In through the bushes, on any foggy day,
My Da would come a-swishing of the drops away,
With a prayer for my death and a groan for my birth,
A-mumbling of his beads for all that he was worth.

And there sit my Ma, her knees beneath her chin,
A-looking in his face and a-drinking of it in,
And a-marking in the moss some funny little saying
That would mean just the opposite of all that he was praying!

He taught me the holy-talk of Vesper and of Matin,
He heard me my Greek and he heard me my Latin,
He blessed me and crossed me to keep my soul from evil,
And we watched him out of sight, and we conjured up the devil!

Oh, the things I haven't seen and the things I haven't known,
What with hedges and ditches till after I was grown,
And yanked both ways by my mother and my father,
With a "Which would you better?" and a "Which would you rather?"

With him for a sire and her for a dam,
What should I be but just what I am?

She is Overhead Singing

Oh, Prue she has a patient man,
    And Joan a gentle lover,
And Agatha's Arth' is a hug-the-hearth,—
    But my true love's a rover!

Mig, her man's as good as cheese
    And honest as a briar,
Sue tells her love what he's thinking of,—
    But my dear lad's a liar!

Oh, Sue and Prue and Agatha
    Are thick with Mig and Joan!
They bite their threads and shake their heads
    And gnaw my name like a bone;

And Prue says, "Mine's a patient man,
    As never snaps me up,"

And Agatha, "Arth' is a hug-the-hearth,
    Could live content in a cup,"

Sue's man's mind is like good jell—
    All one color, and clear—
And Mig's no call to think at all
    What's to come next year,

While Joan makes boast of a gentle lad,
    That's troubled with that and this;—
But they all would give the life they live
    For a look from the man I kiss!

Cold he slants his eyes about,
    And few enough's his choice,—
Though he'd slip me clean for a nun, or a queen,
    Or a beggar with knots in her voice,—

And Agatha will turn awake
    While her good man sleeps sound,
And Mig and Sue and Joan and Prue
    Will hear the clock strike round,

For Prue she has a patient man,
    As asks not when or why,

And Mig and Sue have naught to do
    But peep who's passing by,

Joan is paired with a putterer
    That bastes and tastes and salts,
And Agatha's Arth' is a hug-the-hearth,—
    But my true love is false!

The Prisoner

All right,
Go ahead!
What's in a name?
I guess I'll be locked into
As much as I'm locked out of!

The Unexplorer

There was a road ran past our house
Too lovely to explore.
I asked my mother once—she said
That if you followed where it led
It brought you to the milk-man's door.
(That's why I have not traveled more.)

Grown-Up

Was it for this I uttered prayers
And sobbed and cursed and kicked the stairs,
That now, domestic as a plate,
I should retire at half-past eight?

The Penitent

I had a little Sorrow,
    Born of a little Sin,
I found a room all damp with gloom
    And shut us all within;
And, "Little Sorrow, weep," said I,
"And, Little Sin, pray God to die,
And I upon the floor will lie
    And think how bad I've been!"

Alas for pious planning—
    It mattered not a whit!
As far as gloom went in that room,
    The lamp might have been lit!
My little Sorrow would not weep,

My little Sin would go to sleep—
To save my soul I could not keep
    My graceless mind on it!

So up I got in anger,
    And took a book I had,

And put a ribbon on my hair
    To please a passing lad.

And, "One thing there's no getting by—
I've been a wicked girl," said I;
"But if I can't be sorry, why,
    I might as well be glad!"

Daphne

Why do you follow me?—
Any moment I can be
Nothing but a laurel-tree.

Any moment of the chase
I can leave you in my place
A pink bough for your embrace.

Yet if over hill and hollow
Still it is your will to follow,
I am off;—to heel, Apollo!

Portrait by a Neighbor

Before she has her floor swept
    Or her dishes done,
Any day you'll find her
    A-sunning in the sun!

It's long after midnight
    Her key's in the lock,
And you never see her chimney smoke
    Till past ten o'clock!

She digs in her garden
    With a shovel and a spoon,
She weeds her lazy lettuce
    By the light of the moon.

She walks up the walk
    Like a woman in a dream,

She forgets she borrowed butter
    And pays you back cream!

Her lawn looks like a meadow,
    And if she mows the place
She leaves the clover standing
    And the Queen Anne's lace!

Midnight Oil

Cut if you will, with Sleep's dull knife,
    Each day to half its length, my friend,—
The years that Time takes off my life
    He'll take from off the other end!

The Merry Maid

Oh, I am grown so free from care
    Since my heart broke!
I set my throat against the air,
    I laugh at simple folk!

There's little kind and little fair
    Is worth its weight in smoke
To me, that's grown so free from care
    Since my heart broke!

Lass, if to sleep you would repair
    As peaceful as you woke,
Best not besiege your lover there
    For just the words he spoke
To me, that's grown so free from care
    Since my heart broke!

To Kathleen

Still must the poet as of old,
In barren attic bleak and cold,
Starve, freeze, and fashion verses to
Such things as flowers and song and you;

Still as of old his being give
In Beauty's name, while she may live,
Beauty that may not die as long
As there are flowers and you and song.

To S. M.

    If he should lie a-dying
I am not willing you should go
Into the earth, where Helen went;
She is awake by now, I know.
Where Cleopatra's anklets rust
You will not lie with my consent;
And Sappho is a roving dust;
Cressid could love again; Dido,
Rotted in state, is restless still;
You leave me much against my will.

The Philosopher

And what are you that, missing you,
    I should be kept awake
As many nights as there are days
    With weeping for your sake?

And what are you that, missing you,
    As many days as crawl
I should be listening to the wind
    And looking at the wall?

I know a man that's a braver man
    And twenty men as kind,
And what are you, that you should be
    The one man in my mind?

Yet women's ways are witless ways,
    As any sage will tell,—
And what am I, that I should love
    So wisely and so well?

Four Sonnets

I

Love, though for this you riddle me with darts,
And drag me at your chariot till I die,—
Oh, heavy prince! O, panderer of hearts!—
Yet hear me tell how in their throats they lie
Who shout you mighty: thick about my hair,
Day in, day out, your ominous arrows purr,
Who still am free, unto no querulous care
A fool, and in no temple worshiper!
I, that have bared me to your quiver's fire,

Lifted my face into its puny rain,
Do wreathe you Impotent to Evoke Desire
As you are Powerless to Elicit Pain!
(Now will the god, for blasphemy so brave,
Punish me, surely, with the shaft I crave!)

II

I think I should have loved you presently,
And given in earnest words I flung in jest;
And lifted honest eyes for you to see,
And caught your hand against my cheek and breast;
And all my pretty follies flung aside
That won you to me, and beneath your gaze,
Naked of reticence and shorn of pride,
Spread like a chart my little wicked ways.
I, that had been to you, had you remained,
But one more waking from a recurrent dream,
Cherish no less the certain stakes I gained,
And walk your memory's halls, austere, supreme,
A ghost in marble of a girl you knew
Who would have loved you in a day or two.

III

Oh, think not I am faithful to a vow!
Faithless am I save to love's self alone.
Were you not lovely I would leave you now:
After the feet of beauty fly my own.
Were you not still my hunger's rarest food,
And water ever to my wildest thirst,
I would desert you—think not but I would!—
And seek another as I sought you first.
But you are mobile as the veering air,
And all your charms more changeful than the tide,
Wherefore to be inconstant is no care:

I have but to continue at your side.
So wanton, light and false, my love, are you,
I am most faithless when I most am true.

IV

I Shall forget you presently, my dear,
So make the most of this, your little day,
Your little month, your little half a year,
Ere I forget, or die, or move away,
And we are done forever; by and by
I shall forget you, as I said, but now,
If you entreat me with your loveliest lie
I will protest you with my favorite vow.
I would indeed that love were longer-lived,
And vows were not so brittle as they are,
But so it is, and nature has contrived
To struggle on without a break thus far,—
Whether or not we find what we are seeking
Is idle, biologically speaking.

Second April

SECOND APRIL

Spring

To what purpose, April, do you return again?
Beauty is not enough.
You can no longer quiet me with the redness
Of little leaves opening stickily.
I know what I know.
The sun is hot on my neck as I observe
The spikes of the crocus.
The smell of the earth is good.
It is apparent that there is no death.
But what does that signify?
Not only under ground are the brains of men
Eaten by maggots.
Life in itself
Is nothing,
An empty cup, a flight of uncarpeted stairs.
It is not enough that yearly, down this hill,
April
Comes like an idiot, babbling and strewing flowers.

City Trees

The trees along this city street,
        Save for the traffic and the trains,
Would make a sound as thin and sweet

As trees in country lanes.
And people standing in their shade
    Out of a shower, undoubtedly
Would hear such music as is made
    Upon a country tree.

Oh, little leaves that are so dumb
    Against the shrieking city air,
I watch you when the wind has come,—
    I know what sound is there.

The Blue-Flag in the Bog

God had called us, and we came;
    Our loved Earth to ashes left;
Heaven was a neighbor's house,
    Open flung to us, bereft.
Gay the lights of Heaven showed,
    And 'twas God who walked ahead;
Yet I wept along the road,
    Wanting my own house instead.

Wept unseen, unheeded cried,
    "All you things my eyes have kissed,
Fare you well! We meet no more,
    Lovely, lovely tattered mist!

Weary wings that rise and fall
    All day long above the fire!"—
Red with heat was every wall,
    Rough with heat was every wire—

"Fare you well, you little winds
    That the flying embers chase!
Fare you well, you shuddering day,
    With your hands before your face!

And, ah, blackened by strange blight,
 Or to a false sun unfurled,
Now forevermore goodbye,
 All the gardens in the world!

On the windless hills of Heaven,
 That I have no wish to see,

White, eternal lilies stand,
 By a lake of ebony.

But the Earth forevermore
 Is a place where nothing grows,—
Dawn will come, and no bud break;
 Evening, and no blossom close.

Spring will come, and wander slow
 Over an indifferent land,
Stand beside an empty creek,
 Hold a dead seed in her hand."

God had called us, and we came,
 But the blessed road I trod
Was a bitter road to me,
 And at heart I questioned God.

"Though in Heaven," I said, "be all
 That the heart would most desire,
Held Earth naught save souls of sinners
 Worth the saving from a fire?

Withered grass,—the wasted growing!
 Aimless ache of laden boughs!"
Little things God had forgotten
 Called me, from my burning house.

"Though in Heaven," I said, "be all
      That the eye could ask to see,
All the things I ever knew
      Are this blaze in back of me."

"Though in Heaven," I said, "be all
      That the ear could think to lack,

All the things I ever knew
      Are this roaring at my back."

It was God who walked ahead,
      Like a shepherd to the fold;
In his footsteps fared the weak,
      And the weary and the old,

Glad enough of gladness over,
      Ready for the peace to be,—
But a thing God had forgotten
      Was the growing bones of me.

And I drew a bit apart,
      And I lagged a bit behind,
And I thought on Peace Eternal,
      Lest He look into my mind;

And I gazed upon the sky,
      And I thought of Heavenly Rest,—
And I slipped away like water
      Through the fingers of the blest!

All their eyes were fixed on Glory,
      Not a glance brushed over me;
"Alleluia! Alleluia!"
      Up the road,—and I was free.

And my heart rose like a freshet,
    And it swept me on before,
Giddy as a whirling stick,
    Till I felt the earth once more.

All the Earth was charred and black,
    Fire had swept from pole to pole;

And the bottom of the sea
    Was as brittle as a bowl;

And the timbered mountain-top
    Was as naked as a skull,—
Nothing left, nothing left,
    Of the Earth so beautiful!

"Earth," I said, "how can I leave you?"
    "You are all I have," I said;
"What is left to take my mind up,
    Living always, and you dead?"

"Speak!" I said, "Oh, tell me something!
    Make a sign that I can see!
For a keepsake! To keep always!
    Quick!—before God misses me!"

And I listened for a voice;—
    But my heart was all I heard;
Not a screech-owl, not a loon,
    Not a tree-toad said a word.

And I waited for a sign;—
    Coals and cinders, nothing more;
And a little cloud of smoke
    Floating on a valley floor.

And I peered into the smoke
    Till it rotted, like a fog:—
There, encompassed round by fire,
    Stood a blue-flag in a bog!

Little flames came wading out,
    Straining, straining towards its stem,

But it was so blue and tall
    That it scorned to think of them!

Red and thirsty were their tongues,
    As the tongues of wolves must be,
But it was so blue and tall—
    Oh, I laughed, I cried, to see!

All my heart became a tear,
    All my soul became a tower,
Never loved I anything
    As I loved that tall blue flower!

It was all the little boats
    That had ever sailed the sea,
It was all the little books
    That had gone to school with me;

On its roots like iron claws
    Rearing up so blue and tall,—
It was all the gallant Earth
    With its back against a wall!

In a breath, ere I had breathed,—
    Oh, I laughed, I cried, to see!—
I was kneeling at its side,
    And it leaned its head on me!

Crumbling stones and sliding sand
    Is the road to Heaven now;
Icy at my straining knees
    Drags the awful under-tow;

Soon but stepping-stones of dust
    Will the road to Heaven be,—

Father, Son and Holy Ghost,
    Reach a hand and rescue me!

"There—there, my blue-flag flower;
    Hush—hush—go to sleep;
That is only God you hear,
    Counting up His folded sheep!

Lullabye—lullabye—
    That is only God that calls,
Missing me, seeking me,
    Ere the road to nothing falls!

He will set His mighty feet
    Firmly on the sliding sand;
Like a little frightened bird
    I will creep into His hand;

I will tell Him all my grief,
    I will tell Him all my sin;
He will give me half His robe
    For a cloak to wrap you in.

Lullabye—lullabye—"
    Rocks the burnt-out planet free!—
Father, Son and Holy Ghost,
    Reach a hand and rescue me!

Ah, the voice of love at last!
    Lo, at last the face of light!
And the whole of His white robe
    For a cloak against the night!

And upon my heart asleep
    All the things I ever knew!—

"Holds Heaven not some cranny, Lord,
    For a flower so tall and blue?"

All's well and all's well!
    Gay the lights of Heaven show!
In some moist and Heavenly place
    We will set it out to grow.

Journey

Ah, could I lay me down in this long grass
And close my eyes, and let the quiet wind
Blow over me,—I am so tired, so tired
Of passing pleasant places! All my life,
Following Care along the dusty road,
Have I looked back at loveliness and sighed;
Yet at my hand an unrelenting hand
Tugged ever, and I passed. All my life long
Over my shoulder have I looked at peace;
And now I fain would lie in this long grass
And close my eyes.
        Yet onward!

        Cat-birds call
Through the long afternoon, and creeks at dusk
Are guttural. Whip-poor-wills wake and cry,
Drawing the twilight close about their throats.
Only my heart makes answer. Eager vines

Go up the rocks and wait; flushed apple-trees
Pause in their dance and break the ring for me;
Dim, shady wood-roads, redolent of fern
And bayberry, that through sweet bevies thread
Of round-faced roses, pink and petulant,
Look back and beckon ere they disappear.
Only my heart, only my heart responds.
Yet, ah, my path is sweet on either side
All through the dragging day,—sharp underfoot,
And hot, and like dead mist the dry dust hangs—
But far, oh, far as passionate eye can reach,
And long, ah, long as rapturous eye can cling,

The world is mine: blue hill, still silver lake,
Broad field, bright flower, and the long white road
A gateless garden, and an open path:
My feet to follow, and my heart to hold.

Eel-Grass

No matter what I say,
    All that I really love
Is the rain that flattens on the bay,
    And the eel-grass in the cove;
The jingle-shells that lie and bleach
    At the tide-line, and the trace
Of higher tides along the beach:
    Nothing in this place.

Elegy Before Death

There will be rose and rhododendron
    When you are dead and under ground;
Still will be heard from white syringas
    Heavy with bees, a sunny sound;

Still will the tamaracks be raining
    After the rain has ceased, and still
Will there be robins in the stubble,
    Brown sheep upon the warm green hill.

Spring will not ail nor autumn falter;
    Nothing will know that you are gone,
Saving alone some sullen plough-land
    None but yourself sets foot upon;

Saving the may-weed and the pig-weed
    Nothing will know that you are dead,—
These, and perhaps a useless wagon
    Standing beside some tumbled shed.

Oh, there will pass with your great passing
    Little of beauty not your own,—
Only the light from common water,
    Only the grace from simple stone!

The Bean-Stalk

Ho, Giant! This is I!
I have built me a bean-stalk into your sky!
La,—but it's lovely, up so high!
This is how I came,—I put
Here my knee, there my foot,
Up and up, from shoot to shoot—
And the blessèd bean-stalk thinning
Like the mischief all the time,
Till it took me rocking, spinning,
In a dizzy, sunny circle,
Making angles with the root,
Far and out above the cackle

Of the city I was born in,
Till the little dirty city
In the light so sheer and sunny
Shone as dazzling bright and pretty
As the money that you find
In a dream of finding money—
What a wind! What a morning!—

Till the tiny, shiny city,
When I shot a glance below,
Shaken with a giddy laughter,
Sick and blissfully afraid,
Was a dew-drop on a blade,
And a pair of moments after
Was the whirling guess I made,—
And the wind was like a whip

Cracking past my icy ears,
And my hair stood out behind,
And my eyes were full of tears,
Wide-open and cold,
More tears than they could hold,
The wind was blowing so,
And my teeth were in a row,
Dry and grinning,
And I felt my foot slip,
And I scratched the wind and whined,
And I clutched the stalk and jabbered,
With my eyes shut blind,—
What a wind! What a wind!

Your broad sky, Giant,
Is the shelf of a cupboard;

I make bean-stalks, I'm
A builder, like yourself,
But bean-stalks is my trade,

I couldn't make a shelf,
Don't know how they're made,
Now, a bean-stalk is more pliant—
La, what a climb!

Weeds

White with daisies and red with sorrel
    And empty, empty under the sky!—
Life is a quest and love a quarrel—
    Here is a place for me to lie.
Daisies spring from damnèd seeds,
    And this red fire that here I see
Is a worthless crop of crimson weeds,
    Cursed by farmers thriftily.

But here, unhated for an hour,
    The sorrel runs in ragged flame,
The daisy stands, a bastard flower,
    Like flowers that bear an honest name.

And here a while, where no wind brings
    The baying of a pack athirst,
May sleep the sleep of blessèd things
    The blood too bright, the brow accurst.

Passer Mortuus Est

Death devours all lovely things;
    Lesbia with her sparrow
Shares the darkness,—presently
    Every bed is narrow
Unremembered as old rain
    Dries the sheer libation,
And the little petulant hand
    Is an annotation.

After all, my erstwhile dear,
    My no longer cherished,
Need we say it was not love,
    Now that love is perished?

Pastoral

If it were only still!—
With far away the shrill
Crying of a cock;
Or the shaken bell
From a cow's throat
Moving through the bushes;
Or the soft shock
Of wizened apples falling
From an old tree
In a forgotten orchard
Upon the hilly rock!
Oh, grey hill,
Where the grazing herd

Licks the purple blossom,
Crops the spiky weed!
Oh, stony pasture,
Where the tall mullein
Stands up so sturdy
On its little seed!

Assault

I

I had forgotten how the frogs must sound
After a year of silence, else I think
I should not so have ventured forth alone
At dusk upon this unfrequented road.

II

I am waylaid by Beauty. Who will walk
Between me and the crying of the frogs?
Oh, savage Beauty, suffer me to pass,
That am a timid woman, on her way
From one house to another!

Travel

The railroad track is miles away,
    And the day is loud with voices speaking,
Yet there isn't a train goes by all day
    But I hear its whistle shrieking.
All night there isn't a train goes by,
    Though the night is still for sleep and dreaming,
But I see its cinders red on the sky,
    And hear its engine steaming.

My heart is warm with the friends I make,
    And better friends I'll not be knowing,
Yet there isn't a train I wouldn't take,
    No matter where it's going.

Low-Tide

These wet rocks where the tide has been,
    Barnacled white and weeded brown
And slimed beneath to a beautiful green,
    These wet rocks where the tide went down
Will show again when the tide is high
    Faint and perilous, far from shore,
No place to dream, but a place to die,—
    The bottom of the sea once more.

There was a child that wandered through
    A giant's empty house all day,—
House full of wonderful things and new,
    But no fit place for a child to play.

Song of a Second April

April this year, not otherwise
    Than April of a year ago,
Is full of whispers, full of sighs,
    Of dazzling mud and dingy snow;
    Hepaticas that pleased you so
Are here again, and butterflies.
There rings a hammering all day,
    And shingles lie about the doors;
In orchards near and far away
    The grey wood-pecker taps and bores;
    And men are merry at their chores,
And children earnest at their play.

The larger streams run still and deep,
    Noisy and swift the small brooks run
Among the mullein stalks the sheep
    Go up the hillside in the sun,
    Pensively,—only you are gone,
You that alone I cared to keep.

Rosemary

For the sake of some things
    That be now no more
I will strew rushes
    On my chamber-floor,
I will plant bergamot
    At my kitchen-door.

For the sake of dim things
    That were once so plain
I will set a barrel
    Out to catch the rain,
I will hang an iron pot
    On an iron crane.

Many things be dead and gone
    That were brave and gay;
For the sake of these things
    I will learn to say,
"An it please you, gentle sirs,"
    "Alack!" and "Well-a-day!"

The Poet and His Book

Down, you mongrel, Death!
    Back into your kennel!
I hove stolen breath
    In a stalk of fennel!
You shall scratch and you shall whine
    Many a night, and you shall worry
    Many a bone, before you bury
One sweet bone of mine!
When shall I be dead?
    When my flesh is withered,
And above my head
    Yellow pollen gathered

All the empty afternoon?
    When sweet lovers pause and wonder
    Who am I that lie thereunder,
Hidden from the moon?

This my personal death?—
    That my lungs be failing
To inhale the breath
    Others are exhaling?
This my subtle spirit's end?—
    Ah, when the thawed winter splashes
    Over these chance dust and ashes,
Weep not me, my friend!

Me, by no means dead
    In that hour, but surely
When this book, unread,

    Rots to earth obscurely,
And no more to any breast,
    Close against the clamorous swelling
    Of the thing there is no telling,
Are these pages pressed!
When this book is mould,
    And a book of many
Waiting to be sold
    For a casual penny,
In a little open case,
    In a street unclean and cluttered,
    Where a heavy mud is spattered
From the passing drays,

Stranger, pause and look;
    From the dust of ages

Lift this little book,
    Turn the tattered pages,
Read me, do not let me die!
    Search the fading letters, finding
    Steadfast in the broken binding
All that once was I!

When these veins are weeds,
       When these hollowed sockets
Watch the rooty seeds
       Bursting down like rockets,
And surmise the spring again,
       Or, remote in that black cupboard,
       Watch the pink worms writhing upward
At the smell of rain,

Boys and girls that lie

       Whispering in the hedges,
Do not let me die,
       Mix me with your pledges;
Boys and girls that slowly walk
       In the woods, and weep, and quarrel,
       Staring past the pink wild laurel,
Mix me with your talk,

Do not let me die!
       Farmers at your raking,
When the sun is high,
       While the hay is making,
When, along the stubble strewn,
       Withering on their stalks uneaten,
       Strawberries turn dark and sweeten
In the lapse of noon;

Shepherds on the hills,
       In the pastures, drowsing
To the tinkling bells
       Of the brown sheep browsing;
Sailors crying through the storm;
       Scholars at your study; hunters
       Lost amid the whirling winter's
Whiteness uniform;

Men that long for sleep;
    Men that wake and revel,—
If an old song leap
    To your senses' level
At such moments, may it be
    Sometimes, though a moment only,
    Some forgotten, quaint and homely
Vehicle of me!

Women at your toil,
    Women at your leisure
Till the kettle boil,
    Snatch of me your pleasure,
Where the broom-straw marks the leaf;
    Women quiet with your weeping
    Lest you wake a workman sleeping,
Mix me with your grief!

Boys and girls that steal
    From the shocking laughter
Of the old, to kneel
    By a dripping rafter
Under the discolored eaves,
    Out of trunks with hingeless covers
    Lifting tales of saints and lovers,
Travelers, goblins, thieves,

Suns that shine by night,
    Mountains made from valleys,—
Bear me to the light,
    Flat upon your bellies
By the webby window lie,
    Where the little flies are crawling,—
    Read me, margin me with scrawling,
Do not let me die!

Sexton, ply your trade!
    In a shower of gravel
Stamp upon your spade!
    Many a rose shall ravel,
Many a metal wreath shall rust
    In the rain, and I go singing
    Through the lots where you are flinging
Yellow clay on dust!

Alms

My heart is what it was before,
    A house where people come and go;
But it is winter with your love,
    The sashes are beset with snow.
I light the lamp and lay the cloth,
    I blow the coals to blaze again;
But it is winter with your love,
    The frost is thick upon the pane.

I know a winter when it comes:
    The leaves are listless on the boughs;
I watched your love a little while,
    And brought my plants into the house.

I water them and turn them south,
    I snap the dead brown from the stem;
But it is winter with your love,—
    I only tend and water them.

There was a time I stood and watched
    The small, ill-natured sparrows' fray;
I loved the beggar that I fed,
    I cared for what he had to say,

I stood and watched him out of sight;
    Today I reach around the door
And set a bowl upon the step;
    My heart is what it was before,

But it is winter with your love;
    I scatter crumbs upon the sill,
And close the window,—and the birds
    May take or leave them, as they will.

Inland

People that build their houses inland,
    People that buy a plot of ground
Shaped like a house, and build a house there,
    Far from the sea-board, far from the sound
Of water sucking the hollow ledges,
    Tons of water striking the shore,—
What do they long for, as I long for
    One salt smell of the sea once more?

People the waves have not awakened,
    Spanking the boats at the harbor's head,
What do they long for, as I long for,—
    Starting up in my inland bed,

Beating the narrow walls, and finding
    Neither a window nor a door,
Screaming to God for death by drowning,—
    One salt taste of the sea once more?

To a Poet that Died Young

Minstrel, what have you to do
With this man that, after you,
Sharing not your happy fate,

Sat as England's Laureate?
Vainly, in these iron days,
Strives the poet in your praise,
Minstrel, by whose singing side
Beauty walked, until you died.
Still, though none should hark again,
Drones the blue-fly in the pane,
Thickly crusts the blackest moss,
Blows the rose its musk across,

Floats the boat that is forgot
None the less to Camelot.

Many a bard's untimely death
Lends unto his verses breath;
Here's a song was never sung:
Growing old is dying young.
Minstrel, what is this to you:
That a man you never knew,
When your grave was far and green,
Sat and gossipped with a queen?

Thalia knows how rare a thing
Is it, to grow old and sing;
When a brown and tepid tide
Closes in on every side.
Who shall say if Shelley's gold
Had withstood it to grow old?

Wraith

"Thin Rain, whom are you haunting,
   That you haunt my door?"
— Surely it is not I she's wanting;
   Someone living here before—

"Nobody's in the house but me:
   You may come in if you like and see."
Thin as thread, with exquisite fingers,—
   Have you seen her, any of you?—
Grey shawl, and leaning on the wind,
   And the garden showing through?

Glimmering eyes,—and silent, mostly,
   Sort of a whisper, sort of a purr,

Asking something, asking it over,
   If you get a sound from her.—

Ever see her, any of you?—
   Strangest thing I've ever known,—
Every night since I moved in,
   And I came to be alone.

"Thin Rain, hush with your knocking!
   You may not come in!
This is I that you hear rocking;
   Nobody's with me, nor has been!"

Curious, how she tried the window,—
   Odd, the way she tries the door,—
Wonder just what sort of people
   Could have had this house before . . .

Ebb

I know what my heart is like
   Since your love died:
It is like a hollow ledge
Holding a little pool
   Left there by the tide,
   A little tepid pool,
Drying inward from the edge.

Elaine

Oh, come again to Astolat!
    I will not ask you to be kind.
And you may go when you will go,
    And I will stay behind.
I will not say how dear you are,
    Or ask you if you hold me dear,
Or trouble you with things for you
    The way I did last year.

So still the orchard, Lancelot,
    So very still the lake shall be,
You could not guess—though you should guess—
    What is become of me.

So wide shall be the garden-walk,
    The garden-seat so very wide,
You needs must think—if you should think—
    The lily maid had died.

Save that, a little way away,
    I'd watch you for a little while,
To see you speak, the way you speak,
    And smile,—if you should smile.

Burial

Mine is a body that should die at sea!
    And have for a grave, instead of a grave
Six feet deep and the length of me,
    All the water that is under the wave!
And terrible fishes to seize my flesh,
    Such as a living man might fear,
And eat me while I am firm and fresh,—
    Not wait till I've been dead for a year!

Mariposa

Butterflies are white and blue
In this field we wander through.
Suffer me to take your hand.
Death comes in a day or two.
All the things we ever knew
Will be ashes in that hour,
Mark the transient butterfly,
How he hangs upon the flower.

Suffer me to take your hand.
Suffer me to cherish you
Till the dawn is in the sky.
Whether I be false or true,
Death comes in a day or two.

The Little Hill

Oh, here the air is sweet and still,
    And soft's the grass to lie on;
And far away's the little hill
    They took for Christ to die on.
And there's a hill across the brook,
    And down the brook's another;
But, oh, the little hill they took,—
    I think I am its mother!

The moon that saw Gethsemane,
    I watch it rise and set;
It has so many things to see,
    They help it to forget.

But little hills that sit at home
    So many hundred years,
Remember Greece, remember Rome,
    Remember Mary's tears.

And far away in Palestine,
    Sadder than any other,
Grieves still the hill that I call mine,—
    I think I am its mother!

Doubt no More that Oberon

Doubt no more that Oberon—
Never doubt that Pan
Lived, and played a reed, and ran
After nymphs in a dark forest,
In the merry, credulous days,—
Lived, and led a fairy band
Over the indulgent land!
Ah, for in this dourest, sorest
Age man's eye has looked upon,
Death to fauns and death to fays,
Still the dog-wood dares to raise—
Healthy tree, with trunk and root—

Ivory bowls that bear no fruit,
And the starlings and the jays—
Birds that cannot even sing—
Dare to come again in spring!

Lament

Listen, children:
Your father is dead.
From his old coats
I'll make you little jackets;
I'll make you little trousers
From his old pants.
There'll be in his pockets
Things he used to put there,

Keys and pennies
Covered with tobacco;
Dan shall have the pennies
To save in his bank;
Anne shall have the keys
To make a pretty noise with.
Life must go on,
And the dead be forgotten;
Life must go on,
Though good men die;
Anne, eat your breakfast;
Dan, take your medicine;
Life must go on;
I forget just why.

Exiled

Searching my heart for its true sorrow,
    This is the thing I find to be:
That I am weary of words and people,
    Sick of the city, wanting the sea;
Wanting the sticky, salty sweetness
    Of the strong wind and shattered spray;
Wanting the loud sound and the soft sound
    Of the big surf that breaks all day.

Always before about my dooryard,
    Marking the reach of the winter sea,
Rooted in sand and dragging drift-wood,
    Straggled the purple wild sweet-pea;

Always I climbed the wave at morning,
    Shook the sand from my shoes at night,
That now am caught beneath great buildings,
    Stricken with noise, confused with light.

If I could hear the green piles groaning
    Under the windy wooden piers,
See once again the bobbing barrels,
    And the black sticks that fence the weirs,

If I could see the weedy mussels
    Crusting the wrecked and rotting hulls,
Hear once again the hungry crying
    Overhead, of the wheeling gulls,

Feel once again the shanty straining
    Under the turning of the tide,

Fear once again the rising freshet,
    Dread the bell in the fog outside,—

I should be happy,—that was happy
    All day long on the coast of Maine!
I have a need to hold and handle
    Shells and anchors and ships again!

I should be happy, that am happy
    Never at all since I came here.
I am too long away from water.
    I have a need of water near.

The Death of Autumn

When reeds are dead and a straw to thatch the marshes,
And feathered pampas-grass rides into the wind
Like agèd warriors westward, tragic, thinned
Of half their tribe, and over the flattened rushes,
Stripped of its secret, open, stark and bleak,
Blackens afar the half-forgotten creek,—
Then leans on me the weight of the year, and crushes

My heart. I know that Beauty must ail and die,
And will be born again,—but ah, to see
Beauty stiffened, staring up at the sky!
Oh, Autumn! Autumn!—What is the Spring to me?

Ode to Silence

Aye, but she?
Your other sister and my other soul
Grave Silence, lovelier
Than the three loveliest maidens, what of her?
Clio, not you,
Not you, Calliope,
Nor all your wanton line,
Not Beauty's perfect self shall comfort me
For Silence once departed,
For her the cool-tongued, her the tranquil-hearted,
Whom evermore I follow wistfully,

Wandering Heaven and Earth and Hell and the four seasons through;
Thalia, not you,
Not you, Melpomene,
Not your incomparable feet, O thin Terpsichore,
I seek in this great hall,
But one more pale, more pensive, most beloved of you all.

I seek her from afar.
I come from temples where her altars are,
From groves that bear her name,
Noisy with stricken victims now and sacrificial flame,
And cymbals struck on high and strident faces
Obstreperous in her praise

They neither love nor know,
A goddess of gone days,
Departed long ago,

Abandoning the invaded shrines and fanes
Of her old sanctuary,
A deity obscure and legendary,
Of whom there now remains,
For sages to decipher and priests to garble,
Only and for a little while her letters wedged in marble,
Which even now, behold, the friendly mumbling rain erases,
And the inarticulate snow,
Leaving at last of her least signs and traces
None whatsoever, nor whither she is vanished from these places.

"She will love well," I said,
"If love be of that heart inhabiter,
The flowers of the dead;
The red anemone that with no sound
Moves in the wind, and from another wound
That sprang, the heavily-sweet blue hyacinth,
That blossoms underground,
And sallow poppies, will be dear to her.
And will not Silence know
In the black shade of what obsidian steep
Stiffens the white narcissus numb with sleep?
(Seed which Demeter's daughter bore from home,
Uptorn by desperate fingers long ago,
Reluctant even as she,
Undone Persephone,
An! even as she set out again to grow

In twilight, in perdition's lean and inauspicious loam).
She will love well," I said,
"The flowers of the dead;
Where dark Persephone the winter round,
Uncomforted for home, uncomforted,
Lacking a sunny southern slope in northern Sicily,
With sullen pupils focussed on a dream,
Stares on the stagnant stream

That moats the unequivocable battlements of Hell,
There, there will she be found,
She that is Beauty veiled from men and Music in a swound."

"I long for Silence as they long for breath
Whose helpless nostrils drink the bitter sea;
What thing can be
So stout, what so redoubtable, in Death
What fury, what considerable rage, if only she,
Upon whose icy breast,
Unquestioned, uncaressed,
One time I lay,
And whom always I lack,
Even to this day,
Being by no means from that frigid bosom weaned away,
If only she therewith be given me back?"

I sought her down that dolorous labyrinth,
Wherein no shaft of sunlight ever fell,
And in among the bloodless everywhere
I sought her, but the air,
Breathed many times and spent,
Was fretful with a whispering discontent,
And questioning me, importuning me to tell
Some slightest tidings of the light of day they know no more,
Plucking my sleeve, the eager shades were with me where I went.
I paused at every grievous door,
And harked a moment, holding up my hand,—and for a space
A hush was on them, while they watched my face;
And then they fell a-whispering as before;
So that I smiled at them and left them, seeing she was not there.

I sought her, too,
Among the upper gods, although I knew
She was not like to be where feasting is,
Nor near to Heaven's lord,

Being a thing abhorred
And shunned of him, although a child of his,
(Not yours, not yours; to you she owes not breath,
Mother of Song, being sown of Zeus upon a dream of Death).
Fearing to pass unvisited some place
And later learn, too late, how all the while,
With her still face,
She had been standing there and seen me pass, without a smile,
I sought her even to the sagging board whereat

The stout immortals sat;
But such a laughter shook the mighty hall
No one could hear me say:
Had she been seen upon the Hill that day?
And no one knew at all
How long I stood, or when at last I sighed and went away.

There is a garden lying in a lull
Between the mountains and the mountainous sea,
I know not where, but which a dream diurnal
Paints on my lids a moment till the hull
Be lifted from the kernel
And Slumber fed to me.
Your foot-print is not there, Mnemosene,
Though it would seem a ruined place and after
Your lichenous heart, being full
Of broken columns, caryatides
Thrown to the earth and fallen forward on their jointless knees,
And urns funereal altered into dust
Minuter than the ashes of the dead,
And Psyche's lamp out of the earth up-thrust,
Dripping itself in marble wax on what was once the bed
Of Love, and his young body asleep, but now is dust instead.

There twists the bitter-sweet, the white wisteria
Fastens its fingers in the strangling wall,
And the wide crannies quicken with bright weeds;

There dumbly like a worm all day the still white orchid feeds;
But never an echo of your daughters' laughter
Is there, nor any sign of you at all
Swells fungous from the rotten bough, grey mother of Pieria!

Only her shadow once upon a stone
I saw,—and, lo, the shadow and the garden, too, were gone.

I tell you, you have done her body an ill,
You chatterers, you noisy crew!
She is not anywhere!
I sought her in deep Hell;
And through the world as well;
I thought of Heaven and I sought her there;

Above nor under ground
Is Silence to be found,
That was the very warp and woof of you,
Lovely before your songs began and after they were through!
Oh, say if on this hill
Somewhere your sister's body lies in death,
So I may follow there, and make a wreath
Of my locked hands, that on her quiet breast
Shall lie till age has withered them!
                    (Ah, sweetly from the rest
I see
Turn and consider me
Compassionate Euterpe!)
"There is a gate beyond the gate of Death,

Beyond the gate of everlasting Life,
Beyond the gates of Heaven and Hell," she saith,
"Whereon but to believe is horror!
Whereon to meditate engendereth
Even in deathless spirits such as I
A tumult in the breath,
A chilling of the inexhaustible blood

Even in my veins that never will be dry,
And in the austere, divine monotony
That is my being, the madness of an unaccustomed mood.

This is her province whom you lack and seek;
And seek her not elsewhere.
Hell is a thoroughfare
For pilgrims,—Herakles,
And he that loved Euridice too well,
Have walked therein; and many more than these;
And witnessed the desire and the despair
Of souls that passed reluctantly and sicken for the air;
You, too, have entered Hell,
And issued thence; but thence whereof I speak
None has returned,—for thither fury brings
Only the driven ghosts of them that flee before all things.
Oblivion is the name of this abode: and she is there."

Oh, radiant Song! Oh, gracious Memory!
Be long upon this height

I shall not climb again!
I know the way you mean,—the little night,
And the long empty day,—never to see
Again the angry light,
Or hear the hungry noises cry my brain!
Ah, but she,
Your other sister and my other soul,
She shall again be mine;
And I shall drink her from a silver bowl,
A chilly thin green wine,
Not bitter to the taste,
Not sweet,
Not of your press, oh, restless, clamorous nine,—
To foam beneath the frantic hoofs of mirth—
But savoring faintly of the acid earth,

And trod by pensive feet
From perfect clusters ripened without haste
Out of the urgent heat
In some clear glimmering vaulted twilight under the odorous vine.

Lift up your lyres! Sing on!
But as for me, I seek your sister whither she is gone.

Memorial to D. C.
(Vassar College, 1918)

Prologue

Oh, loveliest throat of all sweet throats,
    Where now no more the music is,
With hands that wrote you little notes
    I write you little elegies!

Epitaph

Heap not on this mound
    Roses that she loved so well;
Why bewilder her with roses,
    That she cannot see or smell?
She is happy where she lies
With the dust upon her eyes.

Prayer to Persephone

Be to her, Persephone,
All the things I might not be;
Take her head upon your knee.
She that was so proud and wild,
Flippant, arrogant and free,

She that had no need of me,
Is a little lonely child
Lost in Hell,—Persephone,
Take her head upon your knee;
Say to her, "My dear, my dear,
It is not so dreadful here."

Chorus

Give away her gowns,
Give away her shoes;
She has no more use
For her fragrant gowns;
Take them all down;
Blue, green, blue,
Lilac, pink, blue,
From their padded hangers;
She will dance no more
In her narrow shoes;
Sweep her narrow shoes
From the closet floor.

Elegy

Let them bury your big eyes
In the secret earth securely,
Your thin fingers, and your fair,
Soft, indefinite-colored hair,—
All of these in some way, surely,
From the secret earth shall rise;
Not for these I sit and stare,
Broken and bereft completely;
Your young flesh that sat so neatly
On your little bones will sweetly

Blossom in the air.
But your voice,—never the rushing
Of a river underground,

Not the rising of the wind
In the trees before the rain,
Not the woodcock's watery call,
Not the note the white-throat utters,
Not the feet of children pushing
Yellow leaves along the gutters
In the blue and bitter fall,
Shall content my musing mind
For the beauty of that sound
That in no new way at all
Ever will be heard again.

Sweetly through the sappy stalk
Of the vigorous weed,
Holding all it held before,
Cherished by the faithful sun,

On and on eternally
Shall your altered fluid run,
Bud and bloom and go to seed;
But your singing days are done;
But the music of your talk
Never shall the chemistry
Of the secret earth restore.
All your lovely words are spoken.
Once the ivory box is broken,
Beats the golden bird no more.

Dirge

Boys and girls that held her dear,
    Do your weeping now;
All you loved of her lies here.

Brought to earth the arrogant brow,
    And the withering tongue
Chastened; do your weeping now.

Sing whatever songs are sung,
    Wind whatever wreath,
For a playmate perished young,

For a spirit spent in death.
Boys and girls that held her dear,
All you loved of her lies here.

Sonnets

I

We talk of taxes, and I call you friend;
Well, such you are,—but well enough we know
How thick about us root, how rankly grow
Those subtle weeds no man has need to tend,
That flourish through neglect, and soon must send
Perfume too sweet upon us and overthrow
Our steady senses; how such matters go
We are aware, and how such matters end.
Yet shall be told no meagre passion here;
With lovers such as we forevermore
Isolde drinks the draught, and Guinevere
Receives the Table's ruin through her door,
Francesca, with the loud surf at her ear,
Lets fall the colored book upon the floor.

II

Into the golden vessel of great song
Let us pour all our passion; breast to breast
Let other lovers lie, in love and rest;

Not we,—articulate, so, but with the tongue
Of all the world: the churning blood, the long
Shuddering quiet, the desperate hot palms pressed
Sharply together upon the escaping guest,
The common soul, unguarded, and grown strong.
Longing alone is singer to the lute;
Let still on nettles in the open sigh
The minstrel, that in slumber is as mute
As any man, and love be far and high,
That else forsakes the topmost branch, a fruit
Found on the ground by every passer-by.

III

Not with libations, but with shouts and laughter
We drenched the altars of Love's sacred grove,
Shaking to earth green fruits, impatient after
The launching of the colored moths of Love.
Love's proper myrtle and his mother's zone
We bound about our irreligious brows,
And fettered him with garlands of our own,
And spread a banquet in his frugal house.
Not yet the god has spoken; but I fear
Though we should break our bodies in his flame,
And pour our blood upon his altar, here
Henceforward is a grove without a name,
A pasture to the shaggy goats of Pan,
Whence flee forever a woman and a man.

IV

Only until this cigarette is ended,
A little moment at the end of all,
While on the floor the quiet ashes fall,
And in the firelight to a lance extended,
Bizarrely with the jazzing music blended,

The broken shadow dances on the wall,
I will permit my memory to recall
The vision of you, by all my dreams attended.
And then adieu,—farewell!—The dream is done.
Yours is a face of which I can forget
The color and the features, everyone,
The words not ever, and the smiles not yet;
But in your day this moment is the sun
Upon a hill, after the sun has set.

V

Once more into my arid days like dew,
Like wind from an oasis, or the sound
Of cold sweet water bubbling underground,
A treacherous messenger, the thought of you
Comes to destroy me; once more I renew
Firm faith in your abundance, whom I found
Long since to be but just one other mound
Of sand, whereon no green thing ever grew.
And once again, and wiser in no wise,
I chase your colored phantom on the air,
And sob and curse and fall and weep and rise
And stumble pitifully on to where,
Miserable and lost, with stinging eyes,
Once more I clasp,—and there is nothing there.

VI

No rose that in a garden ever grew,
In Homer's or in Omar's or in mine,
Though buried under centuries of fine
Dead dust of roses, shut from sun and dew
Forever, and forever lost from view,
But must again in fragrance rich as wine
The grey aisles of the air incarnadine

When the old summers surge into a new.
Thus when I swear, "I love with all my heart,"
'Tis with the heart of Lilith that I swear,
'Tis with the love of Lesbia and Lucrece;
And thus as well my love must lose some part
Of what it is, had Helen been less fair,
Or perished young, or stayed at home in Greece.

VII

When I too long have looked upon your face,
Wherein for me a brightness unobscured
Save by the mists of brightness has its place,
And terrible beauty not to be endured,
I turn away reluctant from your light,
And stand irresolute, a mind undone,
A silly, dazzled thing deprived of sight
From having looked too long upon the sun.
Then is my daily life a narrow room
In which a little while, uncertainly,
Surrounded by impenetrable gloom,
Among familiar things grown strange to me
Making my way, I pause; and feel, and hark,
Till I become accustomed to the dark.

VIII

And you as well must die, beloved dust,
And all your beauty stand you in no stead;
This flawless, vital hand, this perfect head,
This body of flame and steel, before the gust
Of Death, or under his autumnal frost,
Shall be as any leaf, be no less dead
Than the first leaf that fell,—this wonder fled,
Altered, estranged, disintegrated, lost.
Nor shall my love avail you in your hour.

In spite of all my love, you will arise
Upon that day and wander down the air
Obscurely as the unattended flower,
It mattering not how beautiful you were,
Or how belovèd above all else that dies.

IX

Let you not say of me when I am old,
In pretty worship of my withered hands
Forgetting who I am, and how the sands
Of such a life as mine run red and gold
Even to the ultimate sifting dust, "Behold,
Here walketh passionless age!"—for there expands
A curious superstition in these lands,
And by its leave some weightless tales are told.
In me no lenten wicks watch out the night;
I am the booth where Folly holds her fair;
Impious no less in ruin than in strength,
When I lie crumbled to the earth at length,
Let you not say, "Upon this reverend site
The righteous groaned and beat their breasts in prayer."

X

Oh, my belovèd, have you thought of this:
How in the years to come unscrupulous Time,
More cruel than Death, will tear you from my kiss,
And make you old, and leave me in my prime?
How you and I, who scale together yet
A little while the sweet, immortal height
No pilgrim may remember or forget,
As sure as the world turns, some granite night
Shall lie awake and know the gracious flame
Gone out forever on the mutual stone;
And call to mind that on the day you came

I was a child, and you a hero grown?—
And the night pass, and the strange morning break
Upon our anguish for each other's sake!

XI

As to some lovely temple, tenantless
Long since, that once was sweet with shivering brass,
Knowing well its altars ruined and the grass
Grown up between the stones, yet from excess
Of grief hard driven, or great loneliness,
The worshiper returns, and those who pass
Marvel him crying on a name that was,—
So is it now with me in my distress.
Your body was a temple to Delight;
Cold are its ashes whence the breath is fled,
Yet here one time your spirit was wont to move;
Here might I hope to find you day or night,
And here I come to look for you, my love,
Even now, foolishly, knowing you are dead.

XII

Cherish you then the hope I shall forget
At length, my lord, Pieria?—put away
For your so passing sake, this mouth of clay,
These mortal bones against my body set,
For all the puny fever and frail sweat
Of human love,—renounce for these, I say,
The Singing Mountain's memory, and betray
The silent lyre that hangs upon me yet?
Ah, but indeed, someday shall you awake,
Rather, from dreams of me, that at your side
So many nights, a lover and a bride,
But stern in my soul's chastity, have lain,
To walk the world forever for my sake,
And in each chamber find me gone again!

Wild Swans

I looked in my heart while the wild swans went over.
And what did I see I had not seen before?
Only a question less or a question more;
Nothing to match the flight of wild birds flying.
Tiresome heart, forever living and dying,
House without air, I leave you and lock your door.
Wild swans, come over the town, come over
The town again, trailing your legs and crying!

⊰ PART II ⊱

THREE PLAYS OF
EDNA ST. VINCENT MILLAY

ARIA DA CAPO

PERSONS

PIERROT
COLUMBINE
COTHURNUS, MASQUE OF TRAGEDY
THYRSIS ⎫
CORYDON ⎭ SHEPHERDS

ARIA DA CAPO

A PLAY IN ONE ACT

SCENE

A Stage

The curtain rises on a stage set for a Harlequinade, a merry black and white interior. Directly behind the footlights, and running parallel with them, is a long table, covered with a gay black and white cloth, on which is spread a banquet. At the opposite ends of this table, seated on delicate thin-legged chairs with high backs, are PIERROT *and* COLUMBINE, *dressed according to tradition, excepting that* PIERROT *is in lilac, and* COLUMBINE *in pink. They are dining.*

COLUMBINE: Pierrot, a macaroon! I cannot *live* without a macaroon!

PIERROT: My only love,

You are so intense! . . . Is it Tuesday, Columbine?

I'll kiss you if it's Tuesday.

COLUMBINE: It is Wednesday,

If you must know. . . . Is this my artichoke,

Or yours?

PIERROT: Ah, Columbine, as if it mattered!

Wednesday. . . . Will it be Tuesday, then, tomorrow,

By any chance?

COLUMBINE: Tomorrow will be—Pierrot,

That isn't funny!

PIERROT: I thought it rather nice.

Well, let us drink some wine and lose our heads
And love each other.

COLUMBINE: Pierrot, don't you love
Me now?

PIERROT: La, what a woman! How should I know?
Pour me some wine: I'll tell you presently.

COLUMBINE: Pierrot, do you know, I think you drink too much.

PIERROT: Yes, I dare say I do. . . . Or else too little.
It's hard to tell. You see, I am always wanting
A little more than what I have, or else
A little less. There's something wrong. My dear,
How many fingers have you?

COLUMBINE: La, indeed,
How should I know? It always takes me one hand
To count the other with. It's too confusing.
Why?

PIERROT: Why? I am a student, Columbine;
And search into all matters.

COLUMBINE: La, indeed?
Count them yourself, then!

PIERROT: No. Or, rather, *nay*.
'Tis of no consequence. . . . I am become
A painter, suddenly, and you impress me—
Ah, yes! Six orange bull's-eyes, four green pinwheels,
And one magenta jelly-roll, the title
As follows: *Woman Taking in Cheese from Fire-Escape*.

COLUMBINE: Well, I like that! So that is all I've meant
To you!

PIERROT: Hush! All at once I am become
A pianist. I will image you in sound. . . .
On a new scale. . . . Without tonality. . . .
Vivace senza tempo senza tutto. . . .
Title: *Uptown Express at Six o'Clock*.
Pour me a drink.

COLUMBINE: Pierrot, you work too hard.
You need a rest. Come on out into the garden,
And sing me something sad.

PIERROT: Don't stand so near me!
    I am become a socialist. I love
    Humanity; but I hate people. Columbine,
    Put on your mittens, child; your hands are cold.

COLUMBINE: My hands are *not* cold!

PIERROT: Oh, I am sure they are.
    And you must have a shawl to wrap about you,
    And sit by the fire.

COLUMBINE: Why, I'll do no such thing!
    I'm hot as a spoon in a teacup!

PIERROT: Columbine,
    I'm a philanthropist. I know I am,
    Because I feel so restless. Do not scream,
    Or it will be the worse for you!

COLUMBINE: Pierrot,
    My vinaigrette! I cannot *live* without
    My vinaigrette!

PIERROT: My only love, you are
    So fundamental! . . . How would you like to be
    An actress, Columbine? I am become
    Your manager.

COLUMBINE: Why, Pierrot, *I* can't act.

PIERROT: Can't act! Can't act! La, listen to the woman!
    What's that to do with the price of furs? You're blonde,
    Are you not? You have no education, have you?
    Can't act! You underrate yourself, my dear!

COLUMBINE: Yes, I suppose I do.

PIERROT: As for the rest,
    I'll teach you how to cry, and how to die,
    And other little tricks; and the house will love you.
    You'll be a star by five o'clock . . . that is,
    If you will let me pay for your apartment.

COLUMBINE: Let you? Well, that's a good one!
    Ha! Ha! Ha!
    But why?

PIERROT: But why? Well, as to that, my dear,
    I cannot say. It's just a matter of form.

COLUMBINE: Pierrot, I'm getting tired of caviar
  And peacocks' livers. Isn't there something else
  That people eat? Some humble vegetable,
  That grows in the ground?
PIERROT: Well, there are mushrooms.
COLUMBINE: Mushrooms!
  That's so. I had forgotten . . . mushrooms . . . mushrooms. . . .
  I cannot *live* with . . . How do you like this gown?
PIERROT: Not much. I'm tired of gowns that have the waist-line
  About the waist, and the hem around the bottom,
  And women with their breasts in front of them!
  Zut and *ehè!* Where does one go from here!
COLUMBINE: Here's a persimmon, love. You always liked them.
PIERROT: I am become a critic; there is nothing
  I can enjoy. . . . However, set it aside;
  I'll eat it between meals.
COLUMBINE: Pierrot, do you know,
  Sometimes I think you're making fun of me.
PIERROT: My love, by yon black moon, you wrong us both.
COLUMBINE: There isn't a sign of a moon, Pierrot.
PIERROT: Of course not.
  There never was. *Moon*'s just a word to swear by.
  "Mutton!"—now *there's* a thing you can lay the hands on,
  And set the tooth in! Listen, Columbine:
  I always lied about the moon and you.
  Food is my only lust.
COLUMBINE: Well, eat it, then,
  For Heaven's sake, and stop your silly noise!
  I haven't heard the clock tick for an hour.
PIERROT: It's ticking all the same. If you were a fly,
  You would be dead by now. And if I were a parrot,
  I could be talking for a thousand years!
                    Enter COTHURNUS.
PIERROT: Hello, what's this, for God's sake?
  What's the matter?
  Say, whadda you mean? Get off the stage, my friend,
  And pinch yourself, you're walking in your sleep.

COTHURNUS: I never sleep.

PIERROT: Well, anyhow, clear out.
    You don't belong on here. Wait for your own scene!
    Whadda you think this is, a dress-rehearsal?

COTHURNUS: Sir, I am tired of waiting. I will wait
    No longer.

PIERROT: Well, but whadda you going to do?
    The scene is set for me!

COTHURNUS: True, sir; yet I
    Can play the scene.

PIERROT: Your scene is down for later!

COTHURNUS: That, too, is true, sir; but I play it now.

PIERROT: Oh, very well! Anyway, I am tired
    Of black and white. At least, I think I am.

                              [*Exit* COLUMBINE.]

    Yes, I am sure I am. I know what I'll do!
    I'll go and strum the moon, that's what I'll do. . . .
    Unless, perhaps . . . you never can tell . . . I may be,
    You know, tired of the moon. Well, anyway,
    I'll go find Columbine. . . . And when I find her,
    I will address her thus: "Ehè, Pierrette!"—
    There's something in that.

                              [*Exit* PIERROT.]

COTHURNUS: You, Thyrsis! Corydon!
    Where are you?

THYRSIS: [*Off stage.*] Sir, we are in our dressing-room!

COTHURNUS: Come out and do the scene.

CORYDON: [*Off stage.*] You are mocking us!
    The scene is down for later.

COTHURNUS: That is true;
    But we will play it now. I am the scene.
[*Seats himself on high place in back of stage.*]
                    Enter CORYDON *and* THYRSIS.

CORYDON: Sir, we are counting on this little hour.
    We said, "Here is an hour, in which to think
    A mighty thought, and sing a trifling song,
    And look at nothing."—And, behold! The hour,

Even as we spoke, was over, and the act begun,
Under our feet!

THYRSIS: Sir, we are not in the fancy
To play the play. We had thought to play it later.

CORYDON: Besides, this is the setting for a farce.
Our scene requires a wall; we cannot build
A wall of tissue-paper!

THYRSIS: We cannot act
A tragedy with comic properties!

COTHURNUS: Try it and see. I think you'll find you can.
One wall is like another. And regarding
The matter of your insufficient mood,
The important thing is that you speak the lines
And make the gestures. Wherefore I shall remain
Throughout, and hold the prompt-book. Are you ready?

CORYDON-THYRSIS: [*Sorrowfully.*] Sir, we are always ready.

COTHURNUS: Play the play!

[CORYDON *and* THYRSIS *move the table and chairs to one side out of the way, and seat themselves in a half-reclining position on the floor.*]

THYRSIS: How gently in the silence, Corydon,
Our sheep go up the bank. They crop a grass
That's yellow where the sun is out, and black
Where the clouds drag their shadows. Have you noticed
How steadily, yet with what a slanting eye
They graze?

CORYDON: As if they thought of other things.
What say you, Thyrsis, do they only question
Where next to pull? Or do their far minds draw them
Thus vaguely north of west and south of east?

THYRSIS: One cannot say. . . . The black lamb wears its burdocks
As if they were a garland, have you noticed?
Purple and white—and drinks the bitten grass
As if it were a wine.

CORYDON: I've noticed that.
What say you, Thyrsis, shall we make a song
About a lamb that thought himself a shepherd?

THYRSIS: Why, yes! That is why, no. (I have forgotten my line.)

COTHURNUS: [*Prompting.*] "I know a game worth two of that!"

THYRSIS: Oh, yes. . . . I know a game worth two of that!
 Let's gather rocks, and build a wall between us;
 And say that over there belongs to me,
 And over here to you!

CORYDON: Why, very well.
 And say you may not come upon my side
 Unless I say you may!

THYRSIS: Nor you on mine!
 And if you should, 'twould be the worse for you!

[*They weave a wall of colored crêpe paper ribbons from the center front to the center back of the stage, fastening the ends to* COLUMBINE'S *chair in front and to* PIERROT'S *chair in the back.*]

CORYDON: Now there's a wall a man may see across,
 But not attempt to scale.

THYRSIS: An excellent wall.

CORYDON: Come, let us separate, and sit alone
 A little while, and lay a plot whereby
 We may outdo each other.

[*They seat themselves on opposite sides of the wall.*]

PIERROT: [*Off stage.*] Ehè, Pierrette!

COLUMBINE: [*Off stage.*] My name is Columbine!
 Leave me alone!

THYRSIS: [*Coming up to the wall.*] Corydon, after all, and in spite of
 the fact
 I started it myself, I do not like this
 So very much. What is the sense of saying
 I do not want you on my side the wall?
 It is a silly game. I'd much prefer
 Making the little song you spoke of making,
 About the lamb, you know, that thought himself
 A shepherd! What do you say?

[*Pause.*]

CORYDON: [*At wall.*] I have forgotten the line.

COTHURNUS: [*Prompting.*] "How do I know this isn't a trick—"

CORYDON: Oh, yes. . . . How do I know this isn't a trick
    To get upon my land?
THYRSIS: Oh, Corydon,
    You *know* it's not a trick. I do not like
    The game, that's all. Come over here, or let me
    Come over there.
CORYDON: It is a clever trick
    To get upon my land.
[*Seats himself as before.*]
THYRSIS: Oh, very well! [*Seats himself as before. To himself.*] I think I
    never knew a sillier game.
CORYDON: [*Coming to wall.*] Oh, Thyrsis, just a minute! All the water
    Is on your side the wall, and the sheep are thirsty.
    I hadn't thought of that.
THYRSIS: Oh, hadn't you?
CORYDON: Why, what do you mean?
THYRSIS: What do I mean? I mean
    That I can play a game as well as you can.
    And if the pool is on my side, it's on
    My side, that's all.
CORYDON: You mean you'd let the sheep
    Go thirsty?
THYRSIS: Well, they're not my sheep. My sheep
    Have water enough.
CORYDON: *Your* sheep! You are mad, to call them
    Yours—mine—they are all one flock! Thyrsis, you can't mean
    To keep the water from them, just because
    They happened to be grazing over here
    Instead of over there, when we set the wall up?
THYRSIS: Oh, can't I? Wait and see! And if you try
    To lead them over here, you'll wish you hadn't!
CORYDON: I wonder how it happens all the water
    Is on your side. . . . I'll say you had an eye out
    For lots of little things, my innocent friend,
    When I said, "Let us make a song," and you said,
    "I know a game worth two of that!"

COLUMBINE: [*Off stage.*] Pierrot,
D'you know, I think you must be getting old,
Or fat, or something, stupid, anyway!
Can't you put on some other kind of collar?

THYRSIS: You know as well as I do, Corydon,
I never thought anything of the kind.
Don't you?

CORYDON: I *do* not.

THYRSIS: Don't you?

CORYDON: Oh, I suppose so.
Thyrsis, let's drop this, what do you say? It's only
A game, you know . . . we seem to be forgetting
It's only a game . . . a pretty serious game
It's getting to be, when one of us is willing
To let the sheep go thirsty for the sake of it.

THYRSIS: I know it, Corydon.

[*They reach out their arms to each other across the wall.*]

COTHURNUS: [*Prompting.*] "But how do I know—"

THYRSIS: Oh, yes. . . . But how do I know this isn't a trick
To water your sheep, and get the laugh on me?

CORYDON: You can't know, that's the difficult thing about it,
Of course, you can't be sure. You have to take
My word for it. And I know just how you feel.
But one of us has to take a risk, or else,
Why, don't you see? The game goes on forever! . . .
It's terrible, when you stop to think of it. . . .
Oh, Thyrsis, now for the first time I feel
This wall is actually a wall, a thing
Come up between us, shutting you away
From me. . . . I do not know you anymore!

THYRSIS: No, don't say that! Oh, Corydon, I'm willing
To drop it all, if you will! Come on over
And water your sheep! It is an ugly game.
I hated it from the first. . . . How did it start?

CORYDON: I do not know . . . I do not know . . . I think
I am afraid of you! You are a stranger!

I never set eyes on you before! "Come over
And water my sheep," indeed! They'll be more thirsty
Than they are now before I bring them over
Into your land, and have you mixing them up
With yours, and calling them yours, and trying to keep them!
                        Enter COLUMBINE.
COLUMBINE: [*To* COTHURNUS.] Glummy, I want my hat.
THYRSIS: Take it, and go.
COLUMBINE: Take it and go, indeed. Is it my hat,
Or isn't it? Is this my scene, or not?
Take it and go! Really, you know, you two
Are awfully funny!
                                [*Exit* COLUMBINE.]
THYRSIS: Corydon, my friend,
I'm going to leave you now, and whittle me
A pipe, or sing a song, or go to sleep.
When you have come to your senses, let me know.
[*Goes back to where he has been sitting, lies down and sleeps.* CORYDON, *in going back to where he has been sitting, stumbles over bowl of colored confetti and colored paper ribbons.*]
CORYDON: Why, what is this? Red stones—and purple stones—
And stones stuck full of gold! The ground is full
Of gold and colored stones! . . . I'm glad the wall
Was up before I found them! Otherwise,
I should have had to share them. As it is,
They all belong to me. . . . Unless—[*He goes to wall and digs up and down the length of it, to see if there are jewels on the other side.*] None here——
None here—none here—They all belong to me!
[*Sits.*]
THYRSIS: [*Awakening.*] How curious! I thought the little black lamb
Came up and licked my hair; I saw the wool
About its neck as plain as anything!
It must have been a dream. The little black lamb
Is on the other side of the wall, I'm sure.
[*Goes to wall and looks over.* CORYDON *is seated on the ground, tossing the confetti up into the air and catching it.*]

Hello, what's that you've got there, Corydon?

CORYDON: Jewels.

THYRSIS: Jewels? And where did you ever get them?

CORYDON: Oh, over here.

THYRSIS: You mean to say you found them,
    By digging around in the ground for them?

CORYDON: [*Unpleasantly.*] No, Thyrsis,
    By digging down for water for my sheep.

THYRSIS: Corydon, come to the wall a minute, will you?
    I want to talk to you.

CORYDON: I haven't time.
    I'm making me a necklace of red stones.

THYRSIS: I'll give you all the water that you want,
    For one of those red stones, if it's a good one.

CORYDON: Water? What for? What do I want of water?

THYRSIS: Why, for your sheep!

CORYDON: My sheep? I'm not a shepherd!

THYRSIS: Your sheep are dying of thirst.

CORYDON: Man, haven't I told you
    I can't be bothered with a few untidy
    Brown sheep all full of burdocks? I'm a merchant.
    That's what I am! And if I set my mind to it
    I dare say I could be an emperor!
    [*To himself.*] Wouldn't I be a fool to spend my time
    Watching a flock of sheep go up a hill,
    When I have these to play with? When I have these
    To think about? I can't make up my mind
    Whether to buy a city, and have a thousand
    Beautiful girls to bathe me, and be happy
    Until I die, or build a bridge, and name it
    The Bridge of Corydon, and be remembered
    After I'm dead.

THYRSIS: Corydon, come to the wall,
    Won't you? I want to tell you something.

CORYDON: Hush!
    Be off! Be off! Go finish your nap, I tell you!

THYRSIS: Corydon, listen: if you don't want your sheep,
Give them to me.

CORYDON: Be off! Go finish your nap.
A red one—and a blue one—and a red one—
And a purple one—give you my sheep, did you say?
Come, come! What do you take me for, a fool?
I've a lot of thinking to do, and while I'm thinking,
The sheep might just as well be over here
As over there. . . . A blue one—and a red one—

THYRSIS: But they will die!

CORYDON: And a green one—and a couple
Of white ones, for a change.

THYRSIS: Maybe I have
Some jewels on my side.

CORYDON: And another green one—
Maybe, but I don't think so. You see, this rock
Isn't so very wide. It stops before
It gets to the wall. It seems to go quite deep,
However.

THYRSIS: [*With hatred.*] I see.

COLUMBINE: [*Off stage.*] Look, Pierrot, there's the moon.

PIERROT: [*Off stage.*] Nonsense!

THYRSIS: I see.

COLUMBINE: [*Off stage.*] Sing me an old song, Pierrot,
Something I can remember.

PIERROT: [*Off stage.*] Columbine,
Your mind is made of crumbs, like an escallop
Of oysters, first a layer of crumbs, and then
An oystery taste, and then a layer of crumbs.

THYRSIS: [*Searching.*] I find no jewels . . . but I wonder what
The root of this black weed would do to a man
If he should taste it. . . . I have seen a sheep die,
With half the stalk still drooling from its mouth.
'Twould be a speedy remedy, I should think,
For a festered pride and a feverish ambition.
It has a curious root. I think I'll hack it
In little pieces. . . . First I'll get me a drink;

And then I'll hack that root in little pieces
As small as dust, and see what the color is
Inside.
[*Goes to bowl on floor.*]
The pool is very clear. I see
A shepherd standing on the brink, with a red cloak
About him, and a black weed in his hand. . . .
'Tis I.
[*Kneels and drinks.*]
CORYDON: [*Coming to wall.*] Hello, what are you doing, Thyrsis?
THYRSIS: Digging for gold.
CORYDON: I'll give you all the gold
You want, if you'll give me a bowl of water.
If you don't want too much, that is to say.
THYRSIS: Ho, so you've changed your mind? It's different,
Isn't it, when you want a drink yourself?
CORYDON: Of course it is.
THYRSIS: Well, let me see . . . a bowl
Of water, come back in an hour, Corydon.
I'm busy now.
CORYDON: Oh, Thyrsis, give me a bowl
Of water! And I'll fill the bowl with jewels,
And bring it back!
THYRSIS: Be off, I'm busy now.
[*He catches sight of the weed, picks it up and looks at it, unseen by* CORYDON.]
Wait! Pick me out the finest stones you have. . . .
I'll bring you a drink of water presently.
CORYDON: [*Goes back and sits down, with the jewels before him.*]
A bowl of jewels is a lot of jewels.
THYRSIS: [*Chopping up the weed.*] I wonder if it has a bitter taste.
CORYDON: There's sure to be a stone or two among them
I have grown fond of, pouring them from one hand
Into the other.
THYRSIS: I hope it doesn't taste
Too bitter, just at first.
CORYDON: A bowl of jewels
Is far too many jewels to give away

And not get back again.

THYRSIS: I don't believe
He'll notice. He's too thirsty. He'll gulp it down
And never notice.

CORYDON: There ought to be some way
To get them back again. . . . I could give him a necklace,
And snatch it back, after I'd drunk the water,
I suppose. . . . Why, as for that, of course a necklace. . . .

[*He puts two or three of the colored tapes together and tries their strength by pulling them, after which he puts them around his neck and pulls them, gently, nodding to himself. He gets up and goes to the wall, with the colored tapes in his hands.* THYRSIS *in the meantime has poured the powdered root—black confetti—into the pot which contained the flower and filled it up with wine from the punch-bowl on the floor. He comes to the wall at the same time, holding the bowl of poison.*]

THYRSIS: Come, get your bowl of water, Corydon.

CORYDON: Ah, very good! And for such a gift as that
I'll give you more than a bowl of unset stones.
I'll give you three long necklaces, my friend.
Come closer. Here they are.

[*Puts the ribbons about* THYRSIS' *neck.*]

THYRSIS: [*Putting bowl to* CORYDON'S *mouth.*] I'll hold the bowl
Until you've drunk it all.

CORYDON: Then hold it steady.
For every drop you spill I'll have a stone back
Out of this chain.

THYRSIS: I shall not spill a drop.

[CORYDON *drinks, meanwhile beginning to strangle* THYRSIS.]

THYRSIS: Don't pull the string so tight.

CORYDON: You're spilling the water.

THYRSIS: You've had enough—you've had enough—stop pulling
The string so tight!

CORYDON: Why, that's not tight at all . . .
How's this?

THYRSIS: [*Drops bowl.*] You're strangling me! Oh, Corydon!
It's only a game! And you are strangling me!

CORYDON: It's only a game, is it? Yet I believe

You've poisoned me in earnest!

[*Writhes and pulls the strings tighter, winding them about* THYRSIS' *neck.*]

THYRSIS: Corydon!

[*Dies.*]

CORYDON: You've poisoned me in earnest. . . . I feel so cold. . . .
So cold . . . this is a very silly game. . . .
Why do we play it? Let's not play this game
A minute more . . . let's make a little song
About a lamb. . . . I'm coming over the wall,
No matter what you say, I want to be near you. . . .

[*Groping his way, with arms wide before him, he strides through the frail papers of the wall without knowing it, and continues seeking for the wall straight across the stage.*]

Where is the wall?

[*Gropes his way back, and stands very near* THYRSIS *without seeing him; he speaks slowly.*]

There isn't any wall, I think.

[*Takes a step forward, his foot touches* THYRSIS' *body, and he falls down beside him.*]

Thyrsis, where is your cloak? Just give me
A little bit of your cloak! . . .

[*Draws corner of* THYRSIS' *cloak over his shoulders, falls across* THYRSIS' *body, and dies.*]

[COTHURNUS *closes the prompt-book with a bang, arises matter-of-factly, comes down stage, and places the table over the two bodies, drawing down the cover so that they are hidden from any actors on the stage, but visible to the audience, pushing in their feet and hands with his boot. He then turns his back to the audience, and claps his hands twice.*]

COTHURNUS: Strike the scene!

[*Exit* COTHURNUS.]

Enter PIERROT *and* COLUMBINE.

PIERROT: Don't puff so, Columbine!

COLUMBINE: Lord, what a mess
This set is in! If there's one thing I hate
Above everything else, even more than getting my feet wet—
It's clutter! He might at least have left the scene

The way he found it . . . don't you say so, Pierrot?

[*She picks up punch bowl. They arrange chairs as before at ends of table.*]

PIERROT: Well, I don't know. I think it rather diverting
The way it is.

[*Yawns, picks up confetti bowl.*]

Shall we begin?

COLUMBINE: [*Screams.*] My God!
What's that there under the table?

PIERROT: It is the bodies
Of the two shepherds from the other play.

COLUMBINE: [*Slowly.*] How curious to strangle him like that,
With colored paper ribbons.

PIERROT: Yes, and yet
I dare say he is just as dead. [*Pauses. Calls.*] Cothurnus!
Come drag these bodies out of here! We can't
Sit down and eat with two dead bodies lying
Under the table! . . . The audience wouldn't stand for it!

COTHURNUS: [*Off stage.*] What makes you think so?
Pull down the tablecloth
On the other side, and hide them from the house,
And play the farce. The audience will forget.

PIERROT: That's so. Give me a hand there, Columbine.

[PIERROT *and* COLUMBINE *pull down the table cover in such a way that the two bodies are hidden from the house, then merrily set their bowls back on the table, draw up their chairs, and begin the play exactly as before.*]

COLUMBINE: Pierrot, a macaroon, I cannot *live* without a macaroon!

PIERROT: My only love,
You are so intense! . . . Is it Tuesday, Columbine?
I'll kiss you if it's Tuesday.

[*Curtains begin to close slowly.*]

COLUMBINE: It is Wednesday,
If you must know. . . . Is this my artichoke
Or yours?

PIERROT: Ah, Columbine, as if it mattered!
Wednesday. . . . Will it be Tuesday, then, tomorrow,
By any chance? . . .

                              Curtain.

THE LAMP AND THE BELL

PERSONS

Written on the occasion of the Fiftieth Anniversary of the Founding of the Vassar College Alumnæ Association

Dedicated to "1917"

LORENZO, King of Fiori

MARIO, King of Lagoverde

GUIDO, Duke of Versilia, Illegitimate Nephew to Lorenzo

GIOVANNI
LUIGI
ANSELMO } Gentlemen at the Court of Lorenzo
RAFFAELE

FIDELIO, Jester at the Court of Lorenzo

GIUSEPPE, Agent for the Duke's estates

CESCO
HORATIO } Townsmen of Fiori

BEPPO, a little boy, son to Giuliana

RIGO, little boy, son to Leonora

CLERK

MESSENGER

OCTAVIA, Lorenzo's second wife

BEATRICE, "Rose-Red," daughter to Lorenzo by a former marriage

BIANCA, "Snow-White," daughter to Octavia by a former marriage

LAURA
CARLOTTA
FRANCESCA
VIOLA
LILINA
LELA   Ladies at the Court of Lorenzo
ARIANNA
CLAUDIA
CLARA
LUCIA

GRAZIA, Nurse to Beatrice and Bianca
GIULIETTA, Servant to Bianca
"LITTLE SNOW-WHITE"
"LITTLE ROSE-RED"

LEONORA
GIULIANA
CLARA
GIOVANITTA   } Women of Fiori
ANNA
EUGENIA

ELENORA
LUISA   } Little girls, daughters to Leonora

GILDA, a little girl, sister to Beppo
ADELINA, another little girl

NURSE
PIERROT
HARLEQUIN
PANTALOON   } Strolling players
POLICHINEOLL
COLOMBINE

Courtiers, Ladies-in-Waiting, Soldiers, Pages, Musicians, Townspeople, Children

THE LAMP AND THE BELL

ANSELMO *and* LUIGI

ANSELMO: What think you, lies there any truth in the tale
   The King will wed again?
LUIGI: Why not, Anselmo?
   A king is no less lonely than a collier
   When his wife dies. And his young daughter there,
   For all her being a princess, is no less
   A motherless child, and cries herself to sleep
   Night after night, as noisily as any,
   You may be sure.
ANSELMO: A motherless child loves not,
   They say, the second mother. Though the King
   May find him comfort in another face,
   As it is well he should—the child, I fancy,
   Is not so lonely as she is distraught
   With grief for the dead Queen, and will not lightly
   Be parted from her tears.
LUIGI: If tales be true,
   The woman hath a daughter, near the age
   Of his, will be a playmate for the Princess.
                    Curtain.

ACT I

Scene I

A garden of the palace at Fiori; four years later. Discovered seated LAURA, FRANCESCA *and* FIDELIO, LAURA *embroidering,* FIDELIO *strumming his lute,* FRANCESCA *lost in thought.*

LAURA: You—Fool! If there be two chords to your lute,
　　Give us the other for a time!
FRANCESCA: And yet, Laura,
　　I somewhat fancied that soft sound he made.
　　'Twas all on the same tone, but 'twas a sweet tone.
LAURA: 'Tis like you. As for myself, let music change
　　From time to time, or have done altogether.
　　Sing us the song, Fidelio, that you made
　　Last night, a song of flowers, and fair skies,
　　And nightingales, and love.
FIDELIO: I know the song.
　　It is a song of winter.
LAURA: How is that?
FIDELIO: Because it is a song of summer set
　　To a sad tune.
FRANCESCA: [*Sadly.*] Ah, well, so that it be not
　　A song of autumn, I can bear to hear it.
LAURA: In any case, music. I am in a mood for music.
　　I am in a mood where if something be not done
　　To startle me, I shall confess my sins.
　　　　　　　　Enter CARLOTTA.
CARLOTTA: Ha! I will have that woman yet by the hair!
LAURA: What woman, pray, Carlotta?
CARLOTTA: Ho! What woman?
　　Who but that scullery-wench, that onion-monger,
　　That slatternly, pale bakeress, that foul witch,
　　The coroneted Fish Wife of Fiori,
　　Her Majesty, the Queen!
FRANCESCA: Hush—hush—Carlotta!

You could be put to death for less than that!

CARLOTTA: Not I, my duck. When I am put to death
'Twill be for more! Oh, I will have her yet
By the hair!

[*For the first time noticing* FIDELIO.]

Fidelio, if you breathe one word
Of this, I will scratch the Princess into ribbons,
Whom you love better than your wit.

FIDELIO: I' faith,
I did but hear you say you are a fish wife,
And all the world knows that.

LAURA: Fear not, Carlotta,
He is as dumb as a prophet. Every second word
He utters eats the one before it. Speak,
But softly.

CARLOTTA: Nay, 'tis nothing. Nay, by my head,
It is a townful! 'Tis the way she has
Of saying "that should be done like this, and this
Like that"! The woman stirs me to that point
I feel like a carrot in a stew, I boil so
I bump the kettle on all sides!

LAURA: My dear,
Were you as plump as I you would not dare
Become so angry. It would make your stays creak.

CARLOTTA: Well, I am done. Fidelio, play me a dirge
To put me in good spirits. Merry music
Is sure to make me sad.

[FIDELIO *plays. Pause.*]

CARLOTTA: 'Tis curious
A woman like her should have a child like that—
So gentle and so pretty-mannered. Faith,

FIDELIO: Hush! Hush! Here come the prettiest pair of birds
That ever sat together on a bough so close
You could not see the sky between. How now,
Snow-White and Rose-Red! Are you reconciled
One to another?

Enter BEATRICE *and* BIANCA, *with their arms about each other.*

BIANCA: Reconciled, Fidelio?

We had not quarreled!

[*Laughter from* FIDELIO *and the ladies.*]

BEATRICE: Do not listen to him,

Bianca, 'tis but the jingling of his bells.

Fidelio, do you make a better jest than that

At once, or have the clappers cut from them.

FIDELIO: Alas, alas, all the good jests are made.

I made them yesterday.

CARLOTTA: If that be true,

You would best become a wise man for a time,

My friend, there are plenty of wise words not yet said!

FIDELIO: I shall say them all tomorrow.

LAURA: If you do,

You will be stoned to death.

FIDELIO: Not I. No one

Will hear me. Well, I am off. I know an old man

Who does not know the road runs past his house;

And yet his bees make honey.

[*Exit* FIDELIO.]

CARLOTTA: [*Looking after him.*] 'Tis the one wise fool

We have among us.

Enter GRAZIA.

GRAZIA: Oh, here you are, my ducklings!

Always together, like a beggar and a flea!

I looked for you at dinner-time; I forget now

What for; but then 'twas a matter of more weight

Than laying siege to a city, la, how time

Does carry one on! An hour is like an ocean,

The way it separates you from yourself!

[*To* BIANCA *and* BEATRICE.] What do you find to talk about all day?

BEATRICE: We do not talk all day.

CARLOTTA: Nay, 'tis you, Grazia,

That talks all day.

BEATRICE: We ride, and play at tennis.

BIANCA: 'Tis you that ride, Beatrice, I but mount
On a heaving hill, and strive my best to stick there.

GRAZIA: I' faith, I have seen you going forth, you sidewise
Aslant your pretty palfrey; and Her Highness,
As God, my judge, astride the devil himself.

BEATRICE: What, Cupid? La, he's gentle as a kitten!
Though he's a little young, 'tis true, not settled yet
In his mind.

LAURA: As to his mind, 'twere a small matter,
Were he a bit more settled in his legs!

GRAZIA: What did I come here for? I must go back
To where I started, and think of it again!

[*Exit* GRAZIA.]

CARLOTTA: [*Calling after her.*] Are you sure that you remember where
you started?
——The woman hath a head like a sieve.

LAURA: And yet,
You may be sure 'tis nothing more than the thimble
Of the matter she's forgotten. I never knew her
Mislay the thread or the needle of a thing.

BIANCA: We must study now, Beatrice, we indeed must.
We have not opened a book since yesterday.

LAURA: La, as for me, I have not opened a book
Since yesteryear. I'd liefer open a vein!

CARLOTTA: Lessons, troth, I remember well those lessons.
As for what I learned, troth, that's a different matter.

FRANCESCA: 'Tis curious; the things that one remembers
Are foolish things. One does not know at all
Why one remembers them. There was a blackbird
With a broken foot somebody found and tamed
And named Euripides! I can see it now.

CARLOTTA: Some of the silly rhymes we used to write
In the margins of our books, I still remember!

LAURA: And eating sweets behind the covers of them!

FRANCESCA: And faces—faces—faces—and a little game
We used to play, all marching in a row

And singing! I wish I were a child again.

BEATRICE: You are not old, Francesca. You are very young,
And very beautiful!

FRANCESCA: I have been beautiful
Too many years to be so very young.

CARLOTTA: How now, Francesca! Would you have it said
You are enamoured of some beardless youth,
That so you see the wrinkles suddenly?
Have done! Have done!

BIANCA: Where shall we study, Bice?

BEATRICE: Indoors. I cannot study out of doors.

[*Exeunt* BEATRICE *and* BIANCA.]

LAURA: I vow I never knew a pair of lovers
More constant than those two.

CARLOTTA: A pair of lovers?
Marry, I find your figure lacking force!
Since when were lovers true?

FRANCESCA: Oh, peace, Carlotta!
You bear too sharp a weapon against the world,
A split tongue full of poison, in a head
That darts at every heel! I'm going in.

[*Exit* FRANCESCA.]

LAURA: You should not say such things when she is with us, Carlotta.

CARLOTTA: Is the woman in love?

LAURA: In love!
She is so far gone she does not know which way
To sail, all shores are equally out of sight.

[*Exeunt* LAURA *and* CARLOTTA.]

Music off stage. Enter FIDELIO, *singing.*

FIDELIO: "What was I doing when the moon stood above?
What did I do? What did I do?
I lied to a lady that had given me her love,
I swore to be true! I swore to be true!"

[*He picks up from the grass a white scarf which* BEATRICE *was wearing, and
which slipped from her shoulders unnoticed as she went out.*]

My mistress!

[*He thrusts the scarf under his cloak and continues his song, just as* GUIDO
enters from another direction.]
    "And what was I doing when the sun stood above?
    What did I do? What did I do?"
GUIDO: By my sacred word, Fidelio,
    I do not like your song.
FIDELIO: Faith, and small wonder!
    It is a song that sets the evil eye
    To staring in upon itself.
GUIDO: [*Stopping in his walk.*] What mean you
    By that, my throaty friend?
FIDELIO: I mean to say
    That, taking it all in all and by and large,
    You have no ear for music.
GUIDO: I have no ear
    For yours, but it is possible Apollo
    Had a better tenor. I never heard him sing.
FIDELIO: Nay, and how could you? He died when you were born!
GUIDO: He died, that is, in giving birth to me?
FIDELIO: Ay, if you like, you bear as much resemblance
    To him as to your mother's husband, surely.
GUIDO: Take care, Fidelio!
FIDELIO: [*Lightly.*] So! Then it angers you
    Apollo should be deemed your sire! I told you
[*sadly*]
    You have no ear for music!
GUIDO: You are a sly fool,
    My merry friend. What hide you under the cloak?
FIDELIO: Why, 'tis a little patch of snow the sun
    Would lay too hot a hand on.
GUIDO: By my life,
    And what are you that you can keep the sun
    From shining where it will?
FIDELIO: Why, by your life,
    And a foul oath it is! Why, by your life,
    I am a cloud, that is an easy riddle.

Scene II

A garden with a fountain, at Fiori. BEATRICE *and* BIANCA *sitting side by side on a low step. Evening.*

BEATRICE: How beautiful it is to sit like this,
Snow-White, to think of much, and to say little.

BIANCA: Ay, it is beautiful. I shall remember
All my life long these evenings that we spent
Sitting just here, thinking together. [*Pause.*] Rose-Red,
It is four years today since first we met.
Did you know that?

BEATRICE: Nay, is it?

BIANCA: Four years today.
I liked you from the moment that I saw you, Beatrice!

BEATRICE: I you, Bianca. From the very moment!
I thought you were the prettiest little girl
That I had ever seen.

BIANCA: I was afraid
Of you, a little, at first, you were a Princess,
You see. But you explained that being a Princess
Was much the same as anything else. 'Twas nice,
You said, when people were nice, and when they were not nice
'Twas hateful, just the same as everything else.
And then I saw your dolls, and they had noses
All scratched, and wigs all matted, just like mine,
Which reassured me even more! I still, though,
Think of you as a Princess; the way you do things
Is much more wonderful than the way I do them!
The way you speak to the servants, even the way
You pick up something that you drop.

BEATRICE: You goose!
'Tis not because I'm a Princess you feel that way—
I've always thought the same thing about you!
The way you draw your gloves on is to me
More marvelous than the way the sun comes up!

[*They both burst out laughing.*]
    Oh, lud, how droll we are!
BIANCA: Oh, I shall die
    Of laughing! Think you anyone else, Rose-Red,
    Was ever half so silly?
BEATRICE: I dare wager
    There be a thousand, in this realm alone,
    Some even sillier!
BIANCA: Here comes Fidelio!

                Enter FIDELIO.

BEATRICE: Fidelio, sing to us, there is no nightingale
    Abroad tonight, save you. And the night cries
    For music!
BIANCA: Sing, Fidelio!
FIDELIO: I have no thorn
    To lean my breast on. I've been happy all day,
    And happiness ever made a crow of me.
BEATRICE: Sing, none the less, unless you have a cold,
    Which is a singer's only rock of refuge.
    You have no cold, or you would not be happy.
    So sing.
FIDELIO: [*Singing.*] "Oh, little rose-tree, bloom!
           Summer is nearly over.
    The dahlias bleed and the phlox is seed,
           Nothing's left of the clover,
    And the path of the poppy no one knows,
    I would blossom if I were a rose!
    Summer for all your guile
           Will brown in a week to autumn,
    And launched leaves throw a shadow below
           Over the brook's clear bottom,
    And the chariest bud the year can boast
    Be brought to bloom by the chastening frost!
           Oh, little rose-tree, bloom!"
[*As he finishes the song* FIDELIO *goes out, softly strumming the last chords.*
BIANCA *and* BEATRICE *sit quite still for a moment.*]

BIANCA: Do you know what I am thinking, Bice?

BEATRICE: You're wondering where we'll be ten years from now,
Or something of that nature.

BIANCA: Ay, I was wondering
Which would be married first, and go away,
And would we still be friends.

BEATRICE: Oh, do you doubt it, Snow-White?

BIANCA: Nay, nay, I doubt it not, my dear,
But I was wondering. I am suddenly sad,
I know not why. I do not wish to leave you
Ever.

BEATRICE: I know. I cannot bear
To think of parting. We have been happy these four years
Together, have we not?

BIANCA: Oh, Beatrice! [*She weeps.*]

BEATRICE: Nay, do not weep! Come, you must go to bed.
You are tired tonight. We rode too far today.

[*She draws* BIANCA'S *head down to her shoulder.*]
Oh, you are tired, tired, you are very tired.
You must be rocked to sleep, and tucked in bed,
And have your eyelids kissed to make you dream
Of fairies! Come, dear, come.

BIANCA: Oh, I do love you,
Rose-Red! You are so sweet! Oh, I do love you
So much! So much! I never loved anyone
The way that I love you! There is nobody
In all the world so wonderful as you!

[*She throws her arms about* BEATRICE *and clings to her.*]

Scene III

A room in the palace at Fiori. LORENZO *and* BEATRICE *playing chess. Twilight.*

LORENZO: You'll not be able to get out of that,
I think, my girl, with both your castles gone.

BEATRICE: Be not so sure! I have a horse still, father,
And in a strong position: if I move him here,

You lose your bishop; and if you take my bishop,
You lose your queen.

LORENZO: True, but with my two rooks
Set here, where I can push them back and forth,
My king is safe till worms come in and eat him.

BEATRICE: What say you then to this? Will you take this pawn,
Or will you not?

LORENZO: [*Studying the board.*] Od's bones! Where did that come from?

Enter OCTAVIA.

OCTAVIA: La, would you lose your eyesight, both of you!
Fumbling about those chessmen in the dark?
You, Beatrice, at least, should have more wit!

LORENZO: "At least" hm! Did you hear her say, "at least,"
Bice, my daughter?

BEATRICE: Ay. But it is true
The twilight comes before one knows it.

LORENZO: Ay.
'Tis true, but unimportant. Nevertheless,
I am a tractable old fellow. Look you,
I will but stay to map the lay of the pieces
Upon this bit of letter. 'Tis from a king
Who could not tell the bishop from the board,
And yet went blind at forty. A little chess
By twilight, mark you, and all might have been well.

Enter BIANCA.

BIANCA: Oh, I've been looking everywhere for you!

OCTAVIA: [*Drily.*] For me?

BIANCA: Nay, mother, for BEATRICE. Bice,
The rose is out at last upon that bush
That never blossomed before, and it is white
As linen, just as I said 'twould be!

BEATRICE: Why, the bud
Was redder than a radish!

BIANCA: Ay, I know.
But the blossom's white, pure white. Come out and see!

[*Politely.*]
  Would you like to see it, mother?
OCTAVIA: Nay, not now, child.
  Some other time.
BEATRICE: Father, we'll end the game
  Tomorrow; and do you not be scheming at it
  All night!
LORENZO: Nay, I will not unfold the chart.
BEATRICE: But you remember well enough without;
  Promise me not to think of it.
LORENZO: I' faith,
  You are a desperate woman. Ay, I promise.
    [*Exeunt* BIANCA *and* BEATRICE. OCTAVIA *seats herself. Pause.*]
OCTAVIA: I tell you, as I've told you often before, Lorenzo, 'tis not
  good for two young girls
   To be so much together!
LORENZO: As you say,
OCTAVIA: For myself, I must confess
  It seems a natural thing enough, that youth
  Should seek out youth. And if they are better pleased
  Talking together than listening to us,
  I find it not unnatural. What have we
  To say to children? They are as different
  From older folk as fairies are from them.
OCTAVIA: "Talking together," Lorenzo! What have they
  To talk about, save things they might much better
  Leave undiscussed? You know what I mean, lovers,
  And marriage, and all that—if that be all!
  One never knows—it is impossible
  To hear what they are saying; they either speak
  In whispers, or burst out in fits of laughter
  At some incredible nonsense. There is nothing
  So silly as young girls at just that age.
  At just Bianca's age, that is to say.
  As for the other, as for Beatrice,

She's older than Bianca, and I'll not have her
Putting ideas into my daughter's head!
LORENZO: Fear not, my love. Your daughter's head will doubtless,
In its good time, put up its pretty hair,
Chatter, fall dumb, go moping in the rain,
Be turned by flattery, be bowed with weeping,
Grow gray, and shake with palsy over a staff,
All this, my love, as empty of ideas
As even the fondest mother's heart could wish.
OCTAVIA: You mock me, sir?
LORENZO: I am but musing aloud,
As is my fashion. And indeed, my dear,
What is the harm in lovers-and-all-that
That virtuous maidens may not pass the time
With pretty tales about them? After all,
Were it not for the years of looking forward to it
And looking back upon it, love would be
Only the commonest bird-song in the hedge,
And men would have more time to think, and less to think about.
OCTAVIA: That may be. But young girls
Should not be left alone too much together.
They grow too much attached. They grow to feel
They cannot breathe apart. It is unhealthy.
LORENZO: It may be true. But as for me, whom youth
Abandoned long ago, I look on youth
As something fresh and sweet, like a young green tree,
Though the wind bend it double. 'Tis you, 'tis I,
'Tis middle age the fungus settles on.
OCTAVIA: Your head is full of images. You have
No answers. I shall do as I spoke of doing,
And separate them for a little while,
Six months, maybe a year. I shall send Bianca
Away within a fortnight. That will cure them.
I know. I know. Such friendships do not last.
Curtain.

ACT II

Scene I—Four months later

A garden, near the palace at Fiori. The young DUKE GUIDO *is discovered standing with one foot resting on a garden-bench, looking off, lost in thought.*
Enter GIOVANNI.

GIOVANNI: That is a merry face you wear, my Guido!
Now that the young King Mario visits the court
And walks all morning in the woods with the Princess,
Or gives her fencing lessons, upon my word,
You are as gay as a gallows!

GUIDO: She is never
Alone with him. Laura—Carlotta—someone
Is always there.

GIOVANNI: Ah—ah—but even so,
No matter who is there, I tell you, lovers
Are always alone!

GUIDO: Why do you say these things, Giovanni?

GIOVANNI: Because I love you, you lean wolf,
And love to watch you snuff the air. My friend,
There was a time I thought it all ambition
With you, a secret itching to be king—
And not so secret, either—an open plot
To marry a girl who will be Queen some morning.
But now at times I wonder. You have a look
As of a man that's nightly gnawed by rats,
The very visage of a man in love.
Is it not so?

GUIDO: I do not know, Giovanni.
I know I have a passion in my stomach
So bitter I can taste it on my tongue.
She hates me. And her hatred draws me to her
As the moon draws the tide.

GIOVANNI: You are like a cat—
There never was a woman yet that feared you

And shunned you, but you leapt upon her shoulder!
Well, I'll be off. The prettiest girl in Fiori,
Unless it be Her Highness, waits for me
By a fountain. All day long she sells blue plums,
And in the evening what she has left of them
She gives to me! You should love simply, Guido,
As I do.

[*Exit* GIOVANNI. GUIDO *sits on the bench and drops his head in his hand.*]

Enter FRANCESCA.

FRANCESCA: [*Softly.*] Guido! Guido!

GUIDO: Who calls me?

FRANCESCA: Guido!

GUIDO: Francesca! Why do you follow me here? You know
I do not wish to see you!

FRANCESCA: Do not be angry.
'Tis half a week since you have spoken to me,
And more than a week since you have so much as laid
Your hand upon my arm! And do you think,
Loving you as I do, I can do without you,
Forever, Guido, and make no sign at all?
I know you said you did not wish to see me
Ever again, but it was only a quarrel—
And we have quarreled before!

GUIDO: It was not a quarrel.
I am tired of you, Francesca. You are too soft.
You weep too much.

FRANCESCA: I do not weep the less
For having known you.

GUIDO: So; it will save you tears, then,
To know me less.

FRANCESCA: Oh, Guido, how your face
Is changed, I cannot think those are the eyes
That looked into my eyes a month ago!
What's come between us?

GUIDO: Nothing has come between us.
It is the simple snapping of a string

Too often played upon.

FRANCESCA: Ah! But I know

Who snapped it! It will do you little good

To look at her, she'll never look at you!

GUIDO: Be silent a moment! Unless you would be silent longer!

FRANCESCA: Indeed! I shall speak out my mind!

You go beyond yourself! There is proportion

Even in a nature like my own, that's twisted

From too much clinging to a crooked tree!

And this is sure: if you no longer love me,

You shall no longer strike me!

MARIO: [*Off stage.*] Beatrice!

Wait for me! Wait!

BEATRICE: [*Off stage.*] Not I! Who does not run

As fast as I run, shall be left behind me!

GUIDO: They are coming here! I do not wish to see them!

FRANCESCA: Oh, Guido!

[*She follows him off. Exeunt* GUIDO *and* FRANCESCA.]

Enter BEATRICE, *running, followed by* MARIO.

MARIO: Beatrice, you run like a boy!

You whistle like a boy! And upon my word,

You are the only girl I ever played

At jousting with, that did not hold her sword

As if it were a needle! Which of us,

Think you, when we are married, will be King?

BEATRICE: When we are married! Sir, I'll have you know

There's an ogre to be tamed, a gem to be pried

From out a dragon's forehead, and three riddles

To be solved, each tighter than the last, before

A Princess may be wed!

MARIO: Even by a King?

BEATRICE: For Kings the rules are sterner! One more riddle,

And a mirror that will show her always young.

MARIO: And if I do these things, then, will you have me, Rose-Red?

BEATRICE: Maybe. And if you do not do them,

Maybe. Come—I will race you to the bridge!

MARIO: [*Catching her hand.*] Nay, not so fast!
Have you no wish to be
Beside me, ever, that you are forever running
Ahead?
BEATRICE: Indeed, if you would have the truth
It has come into my mind more times than once
It would be sweet to be beside you often.
MARIO: Rose-Red!
BEATRICE: Come—I will race you to the bridge!

[*Exeunt* BEATRICE *and* MARIO.]

Scene II

Courtyard of the palace at Fiori. Entire court assembled. A band of strolling players, with a little stage on wheels, are doing a Harlequinade pantomime to amuse the young KING MARIO, *the guest of honor.* BEATRICE *sits beside him. In this scene the two people who are oblivious to the pantomime are* GUIDO *and* OCTAVIA: GUIDO *is apparently brooding over something. From time to time he looks at* BEATRICE *and* MARIO. *Once, having gazed for some moments at the pair, he looks at* OCTAVIA *and sees that she, too, is looking at them, which seems to satisfy him. The Queen does not take her eyes from the two during the entire scene.* BEATRICE *and* MARIO *do not conduct themselves precisely as lovers, but they are very gay and happy to be in each other's company, apparently.* LORENZO *watches the show with a benign, almost childish interest.*

[*Pantomime begins.*]

GIOVANNI: You, Pierrot, are you not a little thick
For such a sorrowful fellow?
PIERROT: Nay, indeed!
Sorrow may come to all. And 'tis amazing
How much a man may live through and keep fat.

[*Pantomime continues.*]

CARLOTTA: Ho! Now he stumbles! Look you, Pantaloon,
If you were not so learned i' the head
You might know better where to put your feet!
LAURA: [*To* CARLOTTA.] 'Tis curious how it addles a man's bones
To think too much.

CARLOTTA: Nay, truth. Wise men were ever
  Awkward i' the legs.

[*Pantomime continues.*]

RAFFAELE: Have at him, Polichinello.

GIOVANNI: Lay on! Lay on!

ANSELMO: Leave not a nail of him!

GIOVANNI: Dog! Would you have him write a book about you?

LUIGI: Spit him i' the liver! It is his only organ!

BEATRICE: [To MARIO.] Nay, it is cruel. I cannot look at it.

MARIO: It is but play.

BEATRICE: Ay, but 'tis cruel play.
  To be so mocked at! Come, take heart, good Doctor!
  'Tis a noisy fellow, but light withal! Blow at him!

GIOVANNI: [*To* GUIDO.] She has the softest heart that ever I saw
  In a hard woman. It may be, seeing she has pity
  For one rogue, she has pity for another!
  Mark you, my Guido, there is hope yet!

GUIDO: Nay,
  There's not. I have opened up my mind to her,
  And she will none of me.

GIOVANNI: [*Jestingly.*] That was the last thing
  You should have done! Speak, did she give for answer
  She loves the King?

GUIDO: Not she. She gave for answer
  She does not love the Duke.

[*Pantomime continues.*]

ANSELMO: [*To* COLOMBINE.] Ah, pretty lady!

CARLOTTA: La, she is fickle! How she turns from one face
  To another face, and smiles into them all!

FRANCESCA: Oh, ay, but 'tis the Pierrot that she loves.

[*Pantomime continues and comes to a close. All applaud.*]

LUIGI: Well done!

ANSELMO: Bravo!

GIOVANNI: A monstrous lively play!

BEATRICE: Oh, is it over? I would it were not over!

MARIO: And yet it pleased you not!

BEATRICE: When it pleased me not,
  I looked at you.
MARIO: And when I pleased you not?
BEATRICE: I looked at Harlequin. However, I saw him
  But fleetingly. Pray, was he dark or fair?
LUIGI: Laura!
LAURA: Who calls? La, it is only Luigi!
LUIGI: Laura, there'll be a moon tonight.
LAURA: I' faith,
  There was a moon last night.
[*She sighs.*]
LUIGI: At ten o'clock,
  Were I by a certain gate, would you be there?
  What say you?
LAURA: Ay, if weariness overtook me,
  And I could not get further!
CARLOTTA: La, 'tis sundown!
[*In the meantime the crowd has been breaking up and dispersing. The curtain falls on the disappearing spectators and on* PIERROT *and his troupe packing up their wagon to go to the next town.*]

Scene III

Fiori. A garden with a fountain. Evening. Enter OCTAVIA *and Ladies.*
OCTAVIA: It would amuse me if I had a lily
  To carry in my hand. You there, Carlotta!
  You have a long arm, plunge it in the pool
  And fish me forth a lily!
CLAUDIA: Majesty,
  They close at night.
OCTAVIA: Well—we will open them.
CARLOTTA: [*Going to fool and scanning it.*] Go to—I am not a frog!
OCTAVIA: What did you say?
ARIANNA: She says she sees a frog, Your Majesty.
FRANCESCA: [*Aside to* CARLOTTA.] You are mad!
  Can you not keep your tongue in your head?
CARLOTTA: Ay, I can keep it in my cheek. There's one.

God grant it have an eel at the end of it,
I'll give the dame good measure.

        While the ladies are at the fool enter GUIDO.

GUIDO: Greeting, madam!

OCTAVIA: Who greets me? Ah, it is the Duke.
Good even, Guido. You seek an audience with me?

GUIDO: Nay—nay—but if you send away your women,
We shall be more alone.

OCTAVIA: [*After considering him a moment.*] You may leave me now,
Laura, Francesca—all of you—and you would best go in
At an early hour, instead of walking the gardens
All night; I would have you with your wits
About you in the morning.

LAURA: [*Aside.*] Oh, indeed?
You would best go in yourself, lest the dew rust you,
You saucepan!

                        [*Exeunt ladies.*]

OCTAVIA: Now, my good sir, you may speak.

GUIDO: [*As if by way of conversation.*] It is a long time, is it not,
your daughter—
Is absent from the court?

OCTAVIA: Why say you that?

GUIDO: Why, but to pass the time, till she returns?

OCTAVIA: Nay, Guido. That is well enough for some,
But not for me. I know the slant of your fancy;
'Tis not in that direction.

GUIDO: Yet methinks
The sooner she is back again at court
The happier for us both.

OCTAVIA: "Us both"? What "both"?

GUIDO: You, madam, and myself.

OCTAVIA: And why for me?

GUIDO: [*Carefully.*] Why, are you not her mother?

OCTAVIA: Hah! [*Pause.*] Guido,
What festers in your mind? Do you speak out now,
If you await some aid from me.

GUIDO: Madam,
    I have but this to say: if I were a woman
    With a marriageable daughter, and a King rode by,
    I'd have her at the window.
OCTAVIA: So. I thought so.
[*With an entire change of manner.*]
    Guido, what think you, does she love the King,
    I mean Lorenzo's daughter?
GUIDO: Ay, she loves him.
OCTAVIA: And loves he her?
GUIDO: Oh, ay. He loves the moon,
    The wind in the cypress trees, his mother's portrait
    At seventeen, himself, his future children—
    He loves her well enough. But had she blue eyes
    And yellow hair, and were afraid of snakes,
    He yet might love her more.
OCTAVIA: You think so, Guido?
    I am content to learn you of that mind.
    There had occurred to me—sometime ago,
    In fact—a similar fancy. And already
    My daughter is well on her way home.
                         [*Exeunt* GUIDO *and* OCTAVIA.]
            Music. Enter BEATRICE *and* FIDELIO.
[FIDELIO *strums his lute softly throughout the next conversation, up to the*
words "and cease to mock me."]
BEATRICE: Fidelio,
    Were you ever in love?
FIDELIO: I was never out of it.
BEATRICE: But truly?
FIDELIO: Well, I was only out of it
    What time it takes a man to right himself
    And once again lose balance. Ah, indeed,
    'Tis good to be in love. I have often noticed,
    The moment I fall out of love, that moment
    I catch a cold.

BEATRICE: Are you in love, then, now?

FIDELIO: Ay, to be sure.

BEATRICE: Oh! Oh! With whom, Fidelio?
Tell me with whom!

FIDELIO: Why, marry, with yourself,
That are the nearest to me, and by the same troth,
The farthest away.

BEATRICE: Go to, Fidelio!
I am in earnest, and you trifle with me
As if I were a child.

FIDELIO: Are you not a child, then?

BEATRICE: Not anymore.

FIDELIO: How so?

BEATRICE: I am in love.

FIDELIO: Oh—oh—oh, misery, misery, misery, misery!

BEATRICE: Why do you say that?

FIDELIO: Say what?

BEATRICE: "Misery, misery."

FIDELIO: It is a song.

BEATRICE: A song?

FIDELIO: Ay, 'tis a lovesong.
Oh, misery, misery, misery, misery, oh!

BEATRICE: Nay, sweet Fidelio, be not so unkind!
I tell you, for the first time in my life
I am in love! Do you be mannerly now,
And cease to mock me.

FIDELIO: What would you have me do?

BEATRICE: I would have you shake your head, and pat my shoulder,
And smile and say, "Godspeed."

FIDELIO: [Doing, so very tenderly.] Godspeed.

BEATRICE: [Bursting into tears.] I' faith
I do not know if I am happy or sad.
But I am greatly moved. I would Bianca
Were here. I never lacked her near so much
As tonight I do, although I lack her always.

She is a long time gone. If I tell you something,
Will you promise not to tell?
FIDELIO: Nay, I'll not promise,
But I'll not tell.
BEATRICE: Fidelio, I do love so
The King from Lagoverde! I do so love him!
FIDELIO: Godspeed, Godspeed.
BEATRICE: Ay, it is passing strange;
Last week I was a child, but now I am not.
And I begin my womanhood with weeping;
I know not why. La, what a fool I am!
'Tis over. Sing, Fidelio.
FIDELIO: Would you a gay song,
My Princess?
BEATRICE: Ay. And yet—nay, not so gay.
A simple song, such as a country boy
Might sing his country sweetheart. Is it the moon
Hath struck me, do you think? I swear by the moon
I am most melancholy soft, and most
Outrageous sentimental! Sing, dear Fool.
FIDELIO: [*Singing.*]

> Butterflies are white and blue
> In this field we wander through.
> Suffer me to take your hand.
> Death comes in a day or two.
>
> All the things we ever knew
> Will be ashes in that hour.
> Mark the transient butterfly,
> How he hangs upon the flower.
>
> Suffer me to take your hand.
> Suffer me to cherish you
> Till the dawn is in the sky.
> Whether I be false or true,
> Death comes in a day or two.

Curtain.

ACT III

Scene I—The following summer

A field or meadow near Fiori. As the curtain rises voices are heard off stage singing a bridal song.

SONG: *Strew we flowers on their pathway!*
       Bride and bridegroom, go you sweetly.
       There are roses on your pathway.
       Bride and bridegroom, go you sweetly.
       Sweetly live together.

Enter VIOLA, LILINA, LELA, ARIANNA *and* CLAUDIA, *laden with garlands, flowering boughs, and baskets of flowers. They meet* ANSELMO *coming from another direction, also bearing flowers.*

VIOLA: How beautiful, Anselmo! Where did you find them?

ANSELMO: Close by the brook.

LILINA: You gathered all there were?

ANSELMO: Not by one-hundredth part.

LELA: Nay, is it true?
    We must have more of them!

ARIANNA: And are they fragrant
    As well?

ANSELMO: Ay, by my heart, they are so sweet
    I near to fainted climbing the bank with them.

[*The ladies cluster about* ANSELMO *and smell the flowers.*]

LILINA: Oh!

VIOLA: Ah!

CLAUDIA: How drowsily sweet!

LELA: Oh, sweet!

ARIANNA: What fragrance!

    Enter LAURA *and* GIOVANNI, *followed by* CARLOTTA *and* RAFFAELE.

LAURA: La, by my lung! I am as out of breath
    As a babe new-born! Whew! Let me catch the air!

[*She drops her flowers and seats herself beside them.*]

CARLOTTA: [*To the younger ladies and* ANSELMO *by way of greeting.*]
    How hot the sun is getting.

ANSELMO: 'Tis nigh noon,
  I think.
GIOVANNI: 'Tis noon.
CLAUDIA: We must be starting back.
LAURA: Not till I get my breath.
RAFFAELE: Come, I will fan you. [*He fans her with a branch.*]
LAURA: 'Tis good—'tis very good—oh, peace—oh, slumber—
  Oh, all good things! You are a proper youth.
  You are a zephyr. I would have you fan me
  Till you fall dead.
CARLOTTA: I tell you when it comes
  To gathering flowers, much is to be said
  For spreading sheets on the grass, it gives you less
  The backache.
LAURA: Nobly uttered, my sweet bird.
GIOVANNI: Yet brides must have bouquets.
CARLOTTA: And sit at home,
  Nursing complexions, whilst I gather them.
LILINA: [*Running to* CARLOTTA, *along with* LELA *and* VIOLA, *and throwing her arms about her.*]
  Nay, out upon you now, Carlotta! Cease now
  To grumble so, 'tis such a pretty day!
VIOLA: And weddings mean a ball!
LELA: And one may dance all night
  At weddings!
LILINA: Till one needs must dance to bed,
  Because one cannot walk there!
GIOVANNI: And one eats
  Such excellent food!
ANSELMO: And drinks such excellent wine!
CLAUDIA: And seldom will you see a bride and bridegroom
  More beautiful and gracious, of whom garlands
  Do more become.
GIOVANNI: 'Tis so, upon my sword!
  Which I neglected to bring with me—'tis so,
  Upon Anselmo's sword!

CARLOTTA: Nay, look you, Laura!

    You must not fall asleep! [*To* RAFFAELE.] Have done, you devil!

    Is it a poppy that you have there? [*To* LAURA.] Look you,

    We must be starting back! [LAURA *rouses, then falls back again.*]

LAURA: Ay, that we must.

ARIANNA: Where are the others?

ANSELMO: Scattered all about.

    I will call to them. Hola! You fauns and dryads!

    Where are you?

VOICES: Here! Here! Is it time to go?

ANSELMO: Come this way! We are starting back!

VOICES: We are coming!

    We'll come in a moment! I cannot bear to leave

    This place!

GIOVANNI: [*As they enter.*] A thousand greetings, lovely Clara!

    Lucia, a thousand greetings! How now, Luigi!

    I know you, man, despite this soft disguise!

    You are no flower girl!

LUIGI: I am a draught-horse,

    That's what I am, for four unyielding women!

    Were I a flower girl, I'd sell the lot

    For a bit of bread and meat—I am so hungry

    I could eat a butterfly!

CARLOTTA: What ho, Francesca!

    I have not seen you since the sun came up!

FRANCESCA: This is not I, I shall not be myself

    Till it goes down!

LELA: Oh, la, what lovely lilies!

FRANCESCA: Be tender with them—I risked my life to get them!

LILINA: Where were they?

FRANCESCA: Troth, I do not know. I think

    They were in a dragon's mouth.

LAURA: [*Suddenly waking.*] Well, are we going? [*All laugh.*]

LUIGI: No one is going that cannot go afoot.

    I have enough to carry!

LAURA: Nay, take me too!

I am a little thing. What does it matter—
One flower more?

LUIGI: You are a thousand flowers,
Sweet Laura, you are a meadow full of them—
I'll bring a wagon for you.

CARLOTTA: Come. Come home.

[*In the meantime the stage has been filling with girls and men bearing flowers, a multitude of people, in groups and couples, humming the song very softly. As* CARLOTTA *speaks several more people take up the song, then finally the whole Crowd. They move off slowly, singing:* "Strew we flowers on their pathway," *etc.*]

Scene II

BIANCA'S *boudoir in the palace at Fiori.* BIANCA *with a mirror in her hand, having her hair done by a maid. Several maids about, holding perfume-flasks, brushes, and veils, articles of apparel of one sort or another.* BEATRICE *standing beside her, watching.*

BIANCA: Look at me, Rose-Red. Am I pretty enough,
Think you, to marry a King?

BEATRICE: You are too pretty.
There is no justice in it. Marry a cobbler
And make a king of him. It is unequal,
Here is one beggarly boy king in his own right,
And king by right of you.

BIANCA: Mario is not
A beggarly boy! Nay, tell me truly, Beatrice,
What do you think of him?

BEATRICE: La, by my soul!
Have I not told you what I think of him
A thousand times? He is graceful enough, I tell you,
And hath a well-shaped head.

BIANCA: Nay, is that all?

BEATRICE: Nay, hands and feet he hath, like any other.

BIANCA: Oh, out upon you for a surly baggage!
Why will you tease me so? You do not like him,
I think.

BEATRICE: Snow-White! Forgive me! La, indeed,
I was but jesting! By my sacred word,
These brides are serious folk.

BIANCA: I could not bear
To wed a man that was displeasing to you.
Loving him as I do, I could not choose
But wed him, if he wished it, but 'twould hurt me
To think he did not please you.

BEATRICE: Let me, then,
Set your sweet heart at rest. You could not find
In Christendom a man would please me more.

BIANCA: Then I am happy.

BEATRICE: Ay, be happy, child.

BIANCA: Why do you call me child?

BEATRICE: Faith, 'tis the
Season o' the year when I am older than you.
Besides, a bride is always younger than a spinster.

BIANCA: A spinster! Do you come here to me,
Rose-Red,
Whilst I pinch you smartly! You, Arianna, push me
Her Highness over here, that I may pinch her!
[*To* LORETTA.] Nay, is it finished? Ay, 'tis very well.
Though not so well, Loretta, as many a day
When I was doing nothing! Nay, my girl,
'Tis well enough. He will take me as I am
Or leave me as I was. You may come back
In half an hour, if you are grieved about it,
And do it again. But go now, all of you.
I wish to be alone. [*To* BEATRICE.] Not you.
                    [*Exeunt all but* BEATRICE *and* BIANCA.]
Oh, Rose-Red,
I trust 'twill not be long before I see you
As happy as you see me now!

BEATRICE: Indeed,
I could not well be happier than I am.
You do not know, maybe, how much I love you.

BIANCA: Ah, but I do, I have a measure for it!

BEATRICE: Ay, for today you have. But not for long.
They say a bride forgets her friends, she cleaves so
To her new lord. It cannot but be true.
You will be gone from me. There will be much
To drive me from your mind.

BIANCA: Shall I forget, then,
When I am old, I ever was a child?
I tell you I shall never think of you
Throughout my life, without such tenderness
As breaks the heart, and I shall think of you
Whenever I am most happy, whenever I am
Most sad, whenever I see a beautiful thing.
You are a burning lamp to me, a flame
The wind cannot blow out, and I shall hold you
High in my hand against whatever darkness.

BEATRICE: You are to me a silver bell in a tower.
And when it rings I know I am near home.

Scene III

A room in the palace. MARIO *alone. Enter* BEATRICE.

BEATRICE: Mario! I have a message for you! Nay,
You need not hang your head and shun me, Mario,
Because you loved me once a little and now
Love somebody else much more. The going of love
Is no less honest than the coming of it.
It is a human thing.

MARIO: Oh, Beatrice!
What can I say to you?

BEATRICE: Nay, but indeed,
Say nothing. All is said. I need no words
To tell me you have been troubled in your heart,
Thinking of me.

MARIO: What can I say to you!

BEATRICE: I tell you, my dear friend, you must forget
This thing that makes you sad. I have forgotten,

In seeing her so happy, that ever I wished
For happiness myself. Indeed, indeed,
I am much happier in her happiness
Than if it were my own; 'tis doubly dear,
I feel it in myself, yet all the time
I know it to be hers, and am twice glad.

MARIO: I could be on my knees to you a lifetime,
Nor pay you half the homage is your due.

BEATRICE: Pay me no homage, Mario, but if it be
I have your friendship, I shall treasure it.

MARIO: That you will have always.

BEATRICE: Then you will promise me
Never to let her know. I never told her
How it was with us, or that I cherished you
More than another. It was on my tongue to tell her
The moment she returned, but she had seen you
Already on the bridge as she went by,
And had leaned out to look at you, it seems,
And you were looking at her, and the first words
She said, after she kissed me, were, "Oh, sister,
I have looked at last by daylight on the man
I see in my dreams!"

MARIO: [*Tenderly.*] Did she say that?

BEATRICE: [*Drily.*] Ay, that
Was what she said. By which I knew, you see,
My dream was over, it could not but be you.
So that I said no word, but my quick blood
Went suddenly quiet in my veins, and I felt
Years older than Bianca. I drew her head
Down to my shoulder, that she might not see my face,
And she spoke on, and on. You must not tell her,
Even when you both are old and there is nothing
To do but remember. She would be withered
With pity for me. She holds me very dear.

MARIO: I promise it, Rose-Red. And oh, believe me,
I said no word to you last year that is not

As true today! I hold you still the noblest
Of women, and the bravest. I have not changed.
Only last year I did not know I could love
As I love now. Her gentleness has crept so
Into my heart, it never will be out.
That she should turn to me and cling to me
And let me shelter her, is the great wonder
Of the world. You stand alone. You need no shelter,
Rose-Red.

BEATRICE: It may be so.

MARIO: Will you forgive me?

BEATRICE: I had not thought of that. If it will please you,
Ay, surely. And now, the reason for my coming:
I have a message for you, of such vast import
She could not trust it to a liv'ried page,
Or even a courier. She bids me tell you
She loves you still, although you have been parted
Since four o'clock.

MARIO: [*Happily.*] Did she say that?

BEATRICE: Ay, Mario.
I must return to her. It is not long now
Till she will leave me.

MARIO: She will never leave you,
She tells me, in her heart.

BEATRICE: [*Happily.*] Did she say that?

MARIO: Ay, that she did, and I was jealous of you
One moment, till I called myself a fool.

BEATRICE: Nay, Mario, she does not take from you
To give to me; and I am most content
She told you that. I will go now. Farewell, Mario!

MARIO: Nay, we shall meet again, Beatrice!

Scene IV

The ballroom of the palace at Fiori, raised place in back, surmounted by two big chairs, for LORENZO *and* OCTAVIA *to sit while the dance goes on. Dais on one side, well down stage, in full sight of the audience, for* MARIO *and* BIANCA.

As the curtain rises the stage is empty except for FIDELIO, *who sits forlornly on the bottom steps of the raised place in the back of the stage, his lute across his knees, his head bowed upon it. Sound of laughter and conversation, possibly rattling of dishes, of stage, evidently a feast going on.*

LAURA: [*Off stage.*] Be still, or I will heave a plate at you!

LUIGI: [*Off stage.*] Nay, gentle Laura, heave not the wedding crockery
　　At the wedding guest! Behold me on my knees
　　To tell the world I love you like a fool!

LAURA: Get up, you oaf! Or here's a platter of gravy
　　Will add the motley to your folly!

LUIGI: Hold her,
　　Some piteous fop, that liketh not to see
　　Fine linen smeared with goose! Oh, gracious Laura,
　　I never have seen a child sucking an orange
　　But I wished an orange, too. This wedding irks me
　　Because 'tis not mine own. Shall we be married
　　Tuesday or Wednesday?

LAURA: Are you in earnest, Luigi?

LUIGI: Ay, that I am, if never I was before.

LAURA: La, I am lost! I am a married woman!
　　Water! Nay, wine will do! On Wednesday, then.
　　I'll have it as far off as possible.

　　　　Enter from banquet-room GUIDO, GIOVANNI, *and* RAFFAELE.

GIOVANNI: Well met, Fidelio! Give us a song!

FIDELIO: Not I!

GUIDO: Why is this? You, that are dripping with song
　　Weekdays, are dry of music for a wedding?

FIDELIO: I have a headache. Go and sit in a tree,
　　And make your own songs.

RAFFAELE: Nay, Fidelio.
　　String the sweet strings, man!

GIOVANNI: Strike the pretty strings!

GUIDO: Give us the silver strings!

FIDELIO: Nay then, I will that!

[*He tears the strings off the lute and throws them in* GUIDO's *face.*]
　　Here be the strings, my merry gentlemen!

Do you amuse yourselves with tying knots in them
And hanging one another! I have a headache.

> [*He runs off, sobbing.*]

RAFFAELE: What ails him, think you?

GIOVANNI: Troth, I have no notion.

> *Enter* NURSE.

GUIDO: What ho, good Grazia! I hear my uncle
   Is ill again!

GRAZIA: Where heard you that, you raven?

GUIDO: Marry, I forget. Is't true?

GRAZIA: It is as false
   As that you have forgotten where you heard it.
   Were you the heir to his power, which I bless God
   You're not! He'd live to hide the throne from you
   Full many a long day yet! Nay, pretty Guido,
   Your cousin is not yet Queen, and when she is—Faith,
   She weareth a wide petticoat, there'll be
   Scant room for you beside her.

> [*Exit* NURSE *across stage.*]

GUIDO: [*To his companions.*] Nonetheless
   I do believe the king is ill.

RAFFAELE: Who told you?

GUIDO: His wife. She is much exercised about him.

GIOVANNI: 'Tis like enough. This woman would rather lie
   Than have her breakfast served to her in bed.

> [*Exeunt* GUIDO, GIOVANNI, *and* RAFFAELE.]

[*Music. Enter musicians and take places on stage. Enter four pages and take places on either side the door as from the banquet-hall and on either side the throne in the back. Enter King and Queen, that is to say* LORENZO *and* OCTAVIA, LORENZO *apparently quite well, and seat themselves on throne in back. Enter courtiers and ladies,* CARLOTTA *with* ANSELMO, LAURA *with* LUIGI, *etc., and stand in little groups about the stage, laughing and talking together. Enter* BEATRICE *alone, her train held by two pages in black. Enter twelve little Cupids, running, and do a short dance in the center of the room, then rush to the empty dais which is awaiting* MARIO *and* BIANCA, *and cluster about it. Enter* BIANCA *and* MARIO, *she in white and silver, with a deep*]

*sky-blue velvet train six yards long, held up by six silver pages (or Cupids);
he in black and gold, with a purple velvet train of the same length held by six
gold pages (or Cupids). His arm is about her waist, she is leaning back her
head against him and looking up into his face. They come in slowly, talking
softly together, as utterly oblivious of the court, the pages, the music, everything,
as if they were a shepherd and a shepherdess walking through a meadow.
They walk slowly across the stage and seat themselves on the dais. The music
changes, strikes up a gay pavane; the ladies and courtiers dance.* GUIDO,
GIOVANNI, *and* RAFFAELE *re-enter just as the music starts and go up to the
ladies;* GUIDO *goes to* BEATRICE, *and she dances with him. In the midst of
the dance* LORENZO *slips a little sidewise in his chair, his head drops forward
on his chest; he does not move again. Nobody notices for some time. The dance
continues, all who are not dancing watching the dancers, save* OCTAVIA, *who
watches with great pride and affection* BIANCA *and* MARIO, *who in turn are
looking at each other.* OCTAVIA *turns finally to speak to* LORENZO, *stares at
him, touches him, then screams. Music stops in confusion on a discord, dance
breaks up wildly, everybody rushes to throne.*]

Scene V

*The same room later that evening, entirely empty, disordered. Musicians'
benches overturned, for example, a couple of instruments left about, garlands
trampled on the floor, a wing of one of the Cupids clinging to the dais of*
BIANCA *and* MARIO. *Enter* BEATRICE, *weeping, goes to her father's throne
and creeps up into it, with her face toward the back of it and clings there,
sobbing quietly. Enter* BIANCA *and* MARIO.

BIANCA: [*Softly.*] Ay. She is here. I thought she would be here.

There are so many people by his bed

Even now, she cannot be alone with him.

MARIO: Is there no hope?

BIANCA: Nay, there is none. 'Tis over.

He was a kind old man.

MARIO: Come, let us go,

And leave her to herself.

BIANCA: Nay, Mario.

I must not leave her. She will sit like that

All night, unless I bid her come away,
And put her into bed.

MARIO: Will you come to me
After she sleeps?

BIANCA: Ay. If she sleeps.

MARIO: And if not?

BIANCA: I could not leave her.

MARIO: Bianca, do you love me?

BIANCA: Ay, Mario!

MARIO: Ah, but not as I love you!

BIANCA: You do not think that, Mario; you know
How much I love you. But I could not be happy
Thinking of her awake in the darkness, weeping,
And all alone.

MARIO: Oh, my sweet love!

BIANCA: It may be
She will sleep.

MARIO: I shall be waiting for you.

[*They embrace. Exit* MARIO.]

[BIANCA *goes to* BEATRICE *and sits at the foot of the throne, putting her head against* BEATRICE'S *feet.*]

BIANCA: Sister.

[*After a moment* BEATRICE *slowly reaches down her hand, and* BIANCA *takes it.*]

Curtain.

ACT IV

Scene I—Five years later

A marketplace in Fiori, vegetables, fruits, and flowers exposed for sale in little stalls and wagons, crowd of townspeople moving about, talking, laughing, buying. Group of children playing a game in a ring. Supper time.

CHILDREN: One, two, three,
The dough is in the oven!
One, two, three,
The bread is on the board!
One, two, three,

The dough is in the oven!
One, two, three,
The bread is on the board!
One, two, three,
All follow me!

EUGENIA: Good-even, Giovanitta. Those are beautiful
Onions you have there.

GIOVANITTA: Ay, it has been a good year
For onions.

EUGENIA: I am taking seven.

GIOVANITTA: Each year,
You buy another onion!

EUGENIA: Faith, each year
I have another mouth to thrust it in!
Beautiful carrots, too, you have.

GIOVANITTA: Ay, carrots
Are well enough. One cannot complain. 'Tis a good year
For carrots.

CLARA: 'Tis a good year for many things.
Prices are low, but not too low for profit.

GIULIANA: And there are fewer taxes than there once were
On things one cannot live without.

ANNA: 'Tis a good Queen
We have, it must be granted.

GIOVANITTA: Ay, and a wise one.

GILDA: And pretty, too.

GIULIANA: Ho, ho! When did you see her?

GILDA: This morning, mother. I was at the edge of the wood
With Beppo, when they rode by to the hunt,
Talking together, and laughing.

BEPPO: [*Calling from across the stage.*] And the horses
With feet like this!

[*Arching his hands and feet to represent a horse stepping delicately.*]

GILDA: And glittering in the sunshine
In a thousand places, mother! I wanted to tell you
When we returned, but you had gone to the brook

With the linen. They were so near us we could hear them
Talking.

BEPPO: [*Coming up.*] And hear the horses breathe!

ANNA: What said they?

GILDA: Well, one of them said—what was the name?

BEPPO: Anselmo.

GILDA: Oh, ay. She said, "Anselmo, am I getting thinner
Do you think? If I be not thinner than I was at starting,
I shall descend at once! I like not this;
It chatters my teeth."

BEPPO: And then she said—

GILDA: What said she?
Oh, ay, about the boat.

BEPPO: She said, "Next time
I shall go fishing instead of hunting. A boat
Hath a more mannerly gait!"

GILDA: There was one horse, mother,
That was all white! There was not one hair upon him
That was not white!

GIULIANA: And who was riding that horse?

BEPPO: A man. And riding well.

GILDA: He was dressed in green,
And had a yellow beard. And there was a lady
With hair the color of Adelina's, bright
Like fire. She was dressed in blue, and was most beautiful.

BEPPO: And she was mounted on a dappled mare.

GILDA: But, oh, it was the Queen that was more lovely—
Than any of the rest!

GIOVANITTA: How did you know, now,
It was the Queen?

GILDA: Nay, but you could not help
But know! She was not laughing like the rest,
Just smiling; and I would not have been afraid
To toss a flower to her from the wood,
If I had had a flower.

BEPPO: You knew her, though,
   Because she was in scarlet. All the world knows
   She wears a scarlet mantle!
GILDA: Nay, if that were all,
   It might have been the Pope!
BEPPO: I would it had been.
   I never saw the Pope.
GILDA: You never saw
   The Queen until this morning! Mother, she rides
   Clothed like a man, almost!
BEPPO: With sword at side!
GILDA: And, oh, the sword had a jeweled—what is the name of it?
BEPPO: Scabbard, of course!
GILDA: A jeweled scabbard, mother!
   I wish I were a queen.
BEPPO: Ho, you would make
   A proper queen, with that droll nose of yours!
GILDA: I know a boy who likes my nose!
BEPPO: Ho, ho!
   He must be a hunchback!
GIULIANA: You must not tease her, Beppo.
GILDA: I wish I were queen. If I were a queen,
   You would not dare to say my nose is droll.
BEPPO: It would be, all the same.
GIOVANITTA: You should be content
   With what you have, not wish to rise beyond it.
   It is a sin to covet.
GIULIANA: Being a queen,
   My bird, is not all riding to the hunt
   Of a sunny morning.
ANNA: Nay, 'tis riding back
   At times, of a rainy night, to such a burden
   Of cares as simple folk have little mind of.
GILDA: I'd rather have a queen's cares than my own.
BEPPO: Ho, ho! Your cares! What cares have you?

GILDA: I have
    A brother that will be teasing me all times!
    'Tis cares enough for one, I tell you.

ADELINA: [*Across stage.*] Beppo!
    Come help me fetch the milk!

GILDA: Oh, Mister Beppo,
    Your sweetheart calls you! Run and fetch the milk!

LEONORA: [*From a house, coming out.*] Come in to supper, children!

RIGO: Oh, not just yet!

ELENORA: Father's not home yet!

LEONORA: You need not wait for him.

LUISA: May we come out again?

LEONORA: [*Joining other women.*] Ay, for a time.
    Till it gets dark.

RIGO: [*To* LUISA.] 'Tis dark now, almost.

LUISA: Hush!
    She does not know it.

GIULIANA: 'Tis dark now.

LEONORA: Ay, I know.
    I let them play a little after dark
    Sometimes, when the weather's fine. I would not have them
    Afraid of shadows. They think I do not know
    Darkness from light.

ELENORA: There's father now!

RIGO: I see him!

[ELENORA, LUISA, and RIGO *run off the stage and along the path.*]

LEONORA: He is late home today. I cannot think
    What may have held him. 'Twill be deep night already
    In the woods.

CESCO: [*Off stage, harshly.*] Down! Down! Do you run back to
    your mother!
    See you not I am in haste? Hang not upon me!

EUGENIA: La! He is in a temper!

LEONORA: I never knew him
    So out of patience with them.

GIULIANA: He is hungry, maybe.

LEONORA: He is often hungry, but I never knew him
   So out of patience. [*The children come running back. To* ELENORA.]
   Why do you weep, my heart?
LUISA: Father is someone else tonight.
ELENORA: [*Weeping.*] He pushed me!
    Enter CESCO, *with game on his shoulder, or a basket of mushrooms.*
SEVERAL WOMEN: Good-even, Cesco.
CESCO: [*To* LEONORA.] Look you, Leonora,
   Have we a bed fit for a queen to lie in?
LEONORA: Nay, faith! Not we!
GILDA: She can have my bed, mother.
GIULIANA: Ay, true. There is a bed in my house, Cesco.
GIOVANITTA: What will the queen do here?
GIULIANA: I would indeed
   She had let us know that she was coming!
CESCO: The Queen
   Knew not herself. Nor is she coming of herself.
   They are bringing her, on a litter of crossed boughs.
GILDA: She is not *dead?*
CESCO: Nay. Wounded i' the arm
   A little, and in a swoon. But the young King
   Of Lagoverde is no more!
WOMEN: How so?
CESCO: I tell you my two eyes have looked this day
   On a sad and useless thing! A fine lad, young,
   And strong, and beautiful as a lad may be,
   And king of a fair country, thrust from horse
   By a foul blow, and sprawled upon the ground,
   Legs wide asunder, fist full of brown mud,
   Hair in his eyes, most pitiful unkingly!
   Bring me a mug of wine, good wife!

                           LEONORA *goes out.*

GIOVANITTA: You, Gilda!
   There is a queen you would not be tonight,
   I'll warrant you, the Queen of Lagoverde,
   With her two fatherless babes!

EUGENIA: Nay, now, good Cesco,
   What is this matter?
CESCO: You'll know it quick enough.
   They will be bringing the Queen here ere I have breath
   To tell you. They are coming by the road.
   I took the mountain path, and ran.
GIULIANA: I must hasten
   To put fresh sheets on. [*To* GILDA.] Look you, listen well
   If he should talk, and tell me afterwards.
                                        [*Exit.*]
EUGENIA: Here comes Horatio! The boats are in. [*Some children rush
   down to the waterside.*]
   A good day, husband?
HORATIO: Ay, a heavy day.
   What think you of that? A big one, eh? Came in
   With a school of little fish, too greedy that time!
   What happens here? The air is full of breathing!
[*The men come up from the boats with children clinging to them.* BEPPO *and*
ADELINA *return from another direction with the milk.*]
LEONORA: [*Somewhat proudly.*] Cesco will tell you.
CESCO: In a word 'tis this: Today the Queen of Fiori,
   Returning from the hunt, is set upon
   By brigands; whereat the King of Lagoverde,
   Being hunting in that quarter and hearing cries,
   Comes up to give his aid; in rendering which
   He gives his life as well, and at this moment,
   On other men's legs, goes heavily home to supper.
   The Queen of Fiori, wounded, and in a swoon
   Only less deep than death itself, comes this way.
CROWD: Ay, here they come!
                    Enter ANSELMO.
ANSELMO: Make way, make way, good people—
   Fall back a little—leave a clear space—give air!
[*Enter* LAURA *and* FRANCESCA, LUIGI, *several gentlemen, and several
attendants, four of them bearing a litter on which lies* BEATRICE, *in a
scarlet cloak, her hair flowing.* LUIGI *is with* LAURA, *who clings to him.*

If possible to arrange, several of the party may lead on their horses and lead them off across the stage. The litter is set down stage in full sight of the audience. BEPPO *comes down stage near it, as does also, from another direction,* GILDA. GIULIANA *returns.*]

ANSELMO: Who has a bed that we may lay her on?
She cannot leave this place tonight.

GIULIANA: This way, sir.

[*The attendants pick up the litter and go off, the crowd following.*]

GILDA: [*Stealing back.*] Hist, Beppo!

BEPPO: Ay?

GILDA: Heard you not something fall,
When they picked her up again?

BEPPO: Ay, that I did.

GILDA: What was it, think you? [*They search.*]
Nay, 'twas nearer here.

BEPPO: I have it. 'Tis her sword!

GILDA: The Queen's? Ay, truly.
How beautiful!

BEPPO: [*Slowly and with awe drawing it from its scabbard.*]
Look, there is blood on it!

Scene II

A room in the palace at Lagoverde. BIANCA *and her two little daughters discovered at the rise of the curtain, she in a big chair, they at her feet.*

BIANCA: And so the fairy laid a spell on her:
Henceforth she should be ugly as a toad.
But the good fairy, seeing this was done,
And having in no wise power to alter this,
Made all toads beautiful.

LITTLE ROSE-RED: They are not beautiful
Now, mother!

LITTLE SNOW-WHITE: That was in another country!
What country, mother?

[BIANCA, *lost in thought, does not answer.*]

LITTLE ROSE-RED: Where is father, mother?

I have not seen him in so many days!

BIANCA: Father is gone away.

LITTLE ROSE-RED: Will he come back?

BIANCA: Nay. He will not come back. But we shall go
Where he is.

LITTLE SNOW-WHITE: Soon?

BIANCA: God grant it may be soon!
Now—shall we play a game?

Enter OCTAVIA.

OCTAVIA: Bianca

BIANCA: Ay.

OCTAVIA: It is a folly to remain indoors
Like this. You should be out in the sunshine.

BIANCA: Nay.
I have no business with the sunshine.

OCTAVIA: Ah,
My daughter, say not so! The children, then,
They have much need of it, and they have need
Of you, at the same time. Take them without.

BIANCA: I do not wish to be in the sunshine.

LITTLE SNOW-WHITE: Mother,
Come out of doors!

OCTAVIA: You see, now!

BIANCA: Do you run out, dears,
And play at ball. Mother will join you later.

LITTLE ROSE-RED: Where is my ball?

BIANCA: Nay, do you not remember?
We put it in the ear of the stone griffin,
Because he hears too much.

LITTLE ROSE-RED: Ay, so we did!

LITTLE SNOW-WHITE: Come on, Rose-Red!

[Exeunt Children.]

OCTAVIA: It is a curious thing
This friend of yours you rate so monstrous high
Has not come nigh you in your sore affliction!

BIANCA: I beg you not to speak of that again,

Mother. 'Tis the third time today you have said that,
Or hinted at it. And I answer always,
"There is some reason for it," as I should answer
Though you cried daily till the day of doom,
"It is a curious thing!" There is some reason,
There is some good reason why she does not come.
OCTAVIA: Oh, ay, I doubt it not! But there are reasons
And reasons!
BIANCA: And what am I to learn from that?
OCTAVIA: 'Tis scarce by reason of too much love for you
She leaves you friendless in your greatest need.
BIANCA: I cannot say. 'Tis one thing or another.
You have no words can turn me to believe
She has forgotten me, or loves me less.
'Tis a big thing, to leave me thus alone,
And there is some big reason.
OCTAVIA: Ay. Oh, ay.
'Tis possible she grieves for Mario's death
No less than you.
BIANCA: [*Simply.*] Ay, it is possible.
I mind she told me on my marriage-day
She was as happy as I.
OCTAVIA: 'Tis a curious thing,
When he was here she came to see you often,
But now that he is gone comes not at all.
BIANCA: [*Simply.*] Ay, it is curious. [*Catching* OCTAVIA's *expression.*]
BIANCA: Nay, what evil thing
Is in your mind, gives you that evil smile?
OCTAVIA: Only a little thought.
BIANCA: A little thought,
I'll warrant you! You'd have me to believe
She loved my husband?
OCTAVIA: Ay, I know she loved him.
BIANCA: It is a lie!
OCTAVIA: How dare you say I lie!
BIANCA: Oh, do not be so proud! Let us speak truth

At length, a little! We are so garnished up
With courtesies, so over-sauced and seasoned,
We cannot taste each other! Why do you tell me
A thing like that? You have no love for me!

OCTAVIA: [*Weeping.*] I love you too much—you are the only thing
I do love!

BIANCA: Nay, it is not love of me
For my own self. Else would you do the thing
Would make me happiest. You know how I have loved her,
Since we were children. You could not be to me
What she was; one forgets too many things.
You could not know my thought. I loved you dearly,
But you were hard to love; one never knew
Whether you would be hot or cold to touch.
Whilst she and I, oh, we were two young trees
So nearly of a height we had the same world
Ever within our visions! Yet all these years,
Even from the time we first went to Fiori,
You have been bearing me your little tales,
"She had done this and that, she was thus and so,"
Seeking to stir and poison the clear water
Of my deep love for her! And now this thing.
Which is not true. But if it had been true,
It would not be so out of all reason cruel
As that you should have told me of it now.
Nay, do not weep. All day 'tis one of us
Making the other weep. We are two strange,
Unhappy Women. Come, let us be at peace.

[*Pause.* BIANCA *rises suddenly.*]

Mother, farewell a little while. I go now
To her, seeing that she does not come to me.
But not to question her, not to demand,
"How comes it: this? What can you say to that?"
Only to sit beside her, as in the old days,
And let her lay her quiet on my heart.

Scene III

The garden at Fiori, same as in Act I, Scene I. Discovered seated on a stone bench in the sunshine, BEATRICE, *clad in a loose gown, looking very ill.* FIDELIO *sings off stage.*

FIDELIO: [*Singing.*]

> Let the little birds sing,
>> Let the little lambs play.
> Spring is here, and so 'tis spring,
>> But not in the old way.

> I recall a place
>> Where a plum-tree grew,
> There you lifted up your face
>> And blossoms covered you.

> If the little birds sing,
>> And the little lambs play,
> Spring is here, and so 'tis spring,
>> But not in the old way.

BEATRICE: It is a pretty song. There be some things
That even the tortured heart's profoundest anguish
Cannot bring down from their high place. Music
Is one of them.

         Enter GRAZIA *carrying a bowl.*

GRAZIA: Now, will you drink this broth,
Or will you not? I swear upon my shroud—
And 'tis a solemn oath—I never nursed
So vaporous a patient! Come, my bird!

BEATRICE: [*Taking the bowl, then setting it down.*]
Nay, Nurse, I cannot.

GRAZIA: Oh, alackaday!
What shall I do with you? Come now, and drink me
The pretty broth, my dear!

BEATRICE: I will drink it later.

'Tis too hot.

GRAZIA: Ay, and in a moment 'twill be

Too cold! And you'll not drink it! I could cry!

[*Exit* Grazia.]

Enter FIDELIO.

BEATRICE: Fidelio, as you love me, do you drink this,

And quickly, man!

FIDELIO: [*With grief.*] Oh, my dear mistress!

BEATRICE: Drink!

FIDELIO: [*Sadly, drinking.*] I best would leave a little, else she'll know

'Twas never you.

BEATRICE: Ay, so you would. I' faith,

It is a knave's trick, but I cannot touch it.

Go now, Fidelio, ere she come again.

[*Exit* Fidelio.]

Enter BIANCA.

BIANCA: [*Softly.*] Rose-Red. [BEATRICE *looks up and listens, thinking it a dream.*]

BIANCA: Rose-Red, dear sister!

BEATRICE: [*Bowing her head and weeping.*] Oh, my heart!

BIANCA: [*Coming toward her.*] Why do you weep?

BEATRICE: [*Looking up startled and seeing her, jumping to her feet.*] Oh, no! Oh, God above!

Go back! Go back!

BIANCA: [*Amazed, quietly.*] Beatrice, are you mad?

'Tis I, Bianca.

BEATRICE: [*More quietly.*] Ay, I know 'tis you.

And you must go away.

BIANCA: [*Breaking down.*] You are mad, my dear!

BEATRICE: I would I were. For madmen have their moments

Of light into the brain. Hear me, Bianca,

You must return at once to Lagoverde,

And come to me no more, and think of me

No more.

BIANCA: Ay. I will go. But ere I go

Tell me you do not love me. 'Tis apparent
You do not. I but wish to hear the words.

BEATRICE: Nay, that I will not say. It would be well,
To say it, and let it be. But I'll not say it,
It is not true.

BIANCA: You love me still?

BEATRICE: I love you
More than all else on earth. But I have wronged you
So hugely that I cannot think of it
And stand here talking with you—I am ill—[*She staggers.*]
You must pardon me—I have been very ill—

BIANCA: Then it is true?

BEATRICE: [*With a cry as of relief.*] Ay, it is true!
Who told you?

BIANCA: My mother told me. I said it was not true.
But if 'tis true—I pity you, Rose-Red.
I pity him. I pity us all together.

BEATRICE: [*Feverishly.*] Ah, I can see it now! The quiet road
In the deep wood's gathering darkness, the reins loose
On the horses' necks, that nodded, nodded, and we
Speaking from time to time, and glad to think
Of home, and suddenly out of nowhere, fury,
And faces, and long swords, and a great noise!
And even as I reached to draw my sword,
The arm that held the scabbard set on fire,
As if the sleeve were burning! And my horse
Backing into the trees, my hair caught, twisted,
Torn out by the roots! Then from the road behind
A second fury! And I turned, confused,
Outraged with pain, and thrust, and it was Mario!

BIANCA: [*Wildly.*] What are you saying? What are you saying? What
is this
You are telling me? That it was you? Your hand?
Oh, God have mercy upon me! Let me go!

BEATRICE: [*Pitifully, reaching out her arms toward her.*]
Snow-White! Snow-White! Farewell!

BIANCA: [*Without turning.*] Oh, God have mercy!

[*Exit* BIANCA. BEATRICE *falls unconscious to the floor.*]

Curtain.

ACT V

Scene I

A room in the palace at Fiori. ANSELMO *and* LUIGI.

LUIGI: Nay, is that true, Anselmo?

ANSELMO: Ay, 'tis true.
   But no one saw save me. I drew her sword
   Out of his heart and thrust it in its scabbard,
   Where she lay senseless.

LUIGI: Oh, unhappy Queen!

ANSELMO: Ay, she does not forget. Has it not struck you
   She rides no more? Her black horse stands in stable,
   Eating his head off. It is two years now
   Since she has visited Lagoverde; and the Queen
   Of Lagoverde comes not nigh this place.

LUIGI: There's not the reason that there was to come
   Before Octavia's death.

ANSELMO: Nay, 'tis not that.

LUIGI: Think you that Beatrice told her?

ANSELMO: Ay,
   I doubt it not.

LUIGI: 'Tis hard. They were close friends.

ANSELMO: And since that day her hand upon the scepter
   Trembles, and Guido sees. She goes too much
   Among the people, nursing them. She loves them;
   Their griefs are hers, their hearts are hers, as well.
   But Guido has a following in this court
   That hangs upon his word, and he has taught them
   Her gentleness is weakness, and her love
   Faint-hearted womanish whims, till they are eager
   To pull her down, and see a man in place of her.

LUIGI: Her throne is like a raft upon a sea,
 That shifts, and rights itself, and may go down
 At any moment.

ANSELMO: The more especially
 For all these drowning beggars that cling to it,
 Chattering for help. She will not strike them off.

LUIGI: Unhappy Queen. And there's a storm approaching,
 If ever I smelled wind.

ANSELMO: I fear it, Luigi.

> [*Exeunt* ANSELMO *and* LUIGI.]
> *Enter* GUIDO *and* FRANCESCA.

FRANCESCA: How do I know you love her still? I know,
 The way you fall a-tapping with your fingers,
 Or plucking at your eyebrows, if her name
 Be spoken, or she move across the court.
 How do I know? Oh, Guido, have I learned you
 So little, then, in all these bitter years?
 I know you very well.

GUIDO: You know too much.
 I'll have an end of this, I tell you!

FRANCESCA: Ay.
 You've told me that before. An end of what?
 What is this thing you'll put this mighty end to?
 'Fore God I would I knew. Could I but name it,
 I might have power to end it then, myself!

GUIDO: I'll have an end of these soft words at twilight,
 And these bad mornings full of bile! I'll have an end
 Of all this spying on me!

FRANCESCA: [*Gently.*] 'Tis not so.
 I do not spy upon you. But I see you
 Bigger than other men, and your least gesture—
 A giant moving rocks. Oh, Guido, tell me
 You do not love her! Even though I know
 You lie, I will believe you, for I must!

GUIDO: [*Pause.*] Nay, I am done with you. I will tell you nothing.
 Out of my way! I have that on my mind

Would crush your silly skull like the shell of an egg!
Od's body, will you keep your ugly claws
From scratching at my sleeve?
[*He thrusts her roughly aside and rushes out.*]
FRANCESCA: [*Creeping away, sobbing.*] Oh, God—oh, God—
I would whatever it is, that 'twere over.

[*Exit.*]

Enter FIDELIO, *and crosses the stage, singing.*
FIDELIO: [*Singing.*]
Rain comes down
And hushes the town.
And where is the voice that I heard crying?
Snow settles
Over the nettles.
Where is the voice that I heard crying?
Sand at last
On the drifting mast.
And where is the voice that I heard crying?
Earth now
On the busy brow.
And where is the voice that I heard crying?

[*Exit* FIDELIO.]

Scene II

*The courtroom in the palace at Fiori, crowded with restless and expectant
people. The crowd is arranged on both sides of the stage, in such a way that
a broad avenue is left in the middle, leading from the footlights to the back of
the stage and gradually narrowing to a point at* BEATRICE'S *throne. On the
extreme right and left of the stage, along the back of the crowd, stands the guard,
a large body of armed soldiers, at attention, in double row. On either side the
throne stands an armed soldier. As the curtain rises the court is all standing
and looking off stage in a certain direction. Enter the Queen.* BEATRICE, *from
that direction, walks in, looking straight ahead, goes to the throne and seats
herself. The court sits. The clerk begins to read.*
CLERK: The first case to be heard is that of Lisa,

A widow with two small children, who resides
Near the Duke's wood, and has been caught in the act
Of cutting trees there, and hauling them home to burn.

BEATRICE: Stand, Lisa. You are a widow, I am told,
With two small children.

LISA: Ay, Your Majesty,
Two little boys.

BEATRICE: I know another widow, Lisa,
With two small children, but hers are little girls.
Have you been cutting trees on the Duke's land?

LISA: No, Majesty. I could not cut a tree.
I have no ax.

BEATRICE: And are you strong enough
To break a tree with your hands?

LISA: No, Majesty.

BEATRICE: I see. What do you do, then? There must be
Some reason for this plaint.

LISA: I gather wood
That's dead, dried boughs, and underbrush that's been
A long time on the ground, and drag it home.

BEATRICE: Have you a woodpile?

LISA: Nay. I gather enough
Each day for the day's need. I have no time
To gather more.

BEATRICE: And does the dry wood burn
As well as other wood?

LISA: Oh, better!

BEATRICE: I see.
You would as lief, then, have this wood you gather,
This dead wood, as a green tree freshly cut?

LISA: Ay, I would liefer have it, Majesty.
I need a fire quickly. I have no time
To wait for wood to season.

BEATRICE: You may sit down,

LISA: Is the Duke's agent here?

AGENT: Ay, here.

BEATRICE: What is it the Duke's custom to have done
   With this dead wood on his estate?
AGENT: He burns it,
   Your Majesty.
BEATRICE: You mean to say, I think,
   He pays a price to have it gathered and burned.
AGENT: Ay, Majesty.
BEATRICE: Where is it burned?
AGENT: In a clearing.
BEATRICE: And what is cooked upon it?
AGENT: Nothing is cooked.
   The Duke is not a gypsy. [*With irritation.*]
[*Pause. Slight titter in court-room, instantly hushed into profound silence.*]
BEATRICE: [*Evenly.*] If he were,
   He would be shrewder, and not be paying money
   For what this woman is glad to do for naught.
   Nothing is cooked, and nobody is warmed,
   A most unthrifty fire! Do you bid the Duke,
   Until he show me sounder cause for plaint,
   Permit this woman to gather unmolested
   Dead wood in his forest, and bear it home. Lisa,
   Take care you break no half-green boughs. The next case?
CLERK: Is that of Mario, a miller, accused
   Of stealing grain. A baker, by name Pietro,
   Brings this complaint against him.
MESSENGER: [*Rushing in and up to throne.*] Majesty,
   Bianca of Lagoverde lies a-dying,
   And calls for you!
BEATRICE: [*Rising.*] She calls for me?
MESSENGER: Ay, Majesty
[BEATRICE *stands very still a moment, then turns to the townspeople.*]
BEATRICE: [*Earnestly and rapidly.*] You people, do you go now and
   live kindly
   Till I return. I may not stay to judge you;
   Wherefore I set you free. For I would rather
   A knave should go at large than that a just man

Be punished. If there be a knave among you,

Let him live thoughtfully till I return.

[*She steps down from the throne, and is immediately seized by the arm on either side by the two guards who have been standing beside the throne.*]

BEATRICE: Why, what is this, Enrico? [*Looking up at the soldier on her right.*]

Nay, it is not

Enrico! [*Looking to other side.*] Nor is it Pablo! How is this?

[*From each side of the stage one row of the double row of soldiers detaches itself, marches down around the front of the stage and up toward the throne, making an armed alley for the Queen to walk down, and entirely surrounding the crowd.*] Nay, all new faces.

So! Upon my word,

This is a marvelous sight. Do you stand back.

And keep your fingers from me! I see you there,

Angelo! Do not turn your head aside!

And you, Filippo! Is the sick hand better

I bound the bandage on? Is't well enough

To draw a sword against me? Nay, I am sick.

I, that have loved you as your mothers love you—

And you do this to me! Lead me away.

[*The two guards lead out the Queen. Nobody else moves. The townspeople cower and stare. The two little pages that bore her train as she entered remain back of the throne, not knowing what to do. As she goes by them, her train dragging on the ground, the two ragged little boys of* LISA, *the wood-gatherer, run out from the group of citizens, pick up the end of her train, and go out, holding it up, one of them with his arm over his eyes.*]

Scene III

A dungeon. BEATRICE *alone, sitting on a bench, her head bowed in her hands. Enter* GUIDO.

BEATRICE: Guido, is't you!

GUIDO: Ay, it is I, my Queen.

You sent for me, an I mistake not?

BEATRICE: Ay.

Guido, you will not keep me when I tell you

Snow-White is dying and calls my name!

GUIDO: I knew that.

BEATRICE: You knew that, and you hold me here. Oh, Heaven!
  What are you?

GUIDO: I am a man. You should have thought
  Of that before. I could have been your friend
  If it had pleased you. Failing that, I am
  Your enemy. I am too aware of you,
  And have been ever, to hold me in at less.

BEATRICE: GUIDO: I beg of you upon my knees
  To let me go!

GUIDO: And why should I do that?

BEATRICE: For pity's sake!

GUIDO: I do not know the word.

BEATRICE: Then for the sake of my sworn hand and seal
  Upon a paper yielding fair to you
  This sovereignty you prize. It is to me
  Little enough tonight. I give it gladly.

GUIDO: You have no power to give what I have taken
  Already, and hold upon my hand, Rose-Red.

BEATRICE: Oh, do not speak that name! Oh,
  Guido, Guido,
  I cannot suffer further! Let me go!
  If only for a moment, let me go!
  I will return, I will but take her hand,
  And come away! I swear it! Let me go!

GUIDO: On one condition only.

BEATRICE: Ay! 'Tis granted,
  Ere it is spoken!

GUIDO: That upon returning
  You come to me, and give yourself to me,
  To lie in my arms lovingly. [*She is stricken speechless.*] You hear?
  To lie in my arms lovingly.

BEATRICE: Oh, God!

GUIDO: It is my only word.

BEATRICE: Oh, God! Oh, God!

GUIDO: 'Tis granted?

BEATRICE: Nay, I cannot! I will die
　　Instead. Oh, God, to think that she will lie there
　　And call for me, and I will never come!
GUIDO: Good night. [*He goes to door.*]
BEATRICE: [*In a quiet voice.*] Guido!
　　It shall be as you say.
GUIDO: [*Rushing to her.*] Ah, Beatrice!
BEATRICE: Nay, touch me not yet.
　　I will return. [*She laughs like a child.*] Why, 'tis a simple matter!
　　I wonder now that even for a moment
　　I held myself so dear! When for her sake
　　All things are little things! This foolish body,
　　This body is not I! There is no I,
　　Saving the need I have to go to her!

Scene IV

A room at Lagoverde. BIANCA *lying in bed, ill to death. The children clinging
to the bed, their nurse trying to draw them away.* GIULIETTA, *a maid, in the
background. Possibly other attendants about.*

LITTLE ROSE-RED: Finish the story, mother!
NURSE: Come away, now!
LITTLE SNOW-WHITE: Finish the story!
BIANCA: Do you go away with nurse
　　A little while. You will bring them back to me
　　Later?
NURSE: [*Weeping.*] Ay, madam. [*She goes out with the children.*]
BIANCA: Later—not much later,
　　I think. Hear you no sound of horses yet,
　　Giulietta, galloping this way?
GIULIETTA: Nay, not yet.
BIANCA: [*To herself.*] I will not go until she comes.
　　I will not.
　　Still, if I should—Giulietta!
GIULIETTA: [*Coming quickly to the bed.*] Ay, my mistress!
BIANCA: She will come, I tell you!
GIULIETTA: Ay, I doubt it not.

BIANCA: Ay, she will come. But if she should come late,
   And I no longer be here to receive her,
   Show her all courtesy, I conjure you.
   She will be weary, and mightily distraught.
   Make her take wine, and bring the children to her.
   And tell her they are hers now. She is their mother.
[GIULIETTA *starts to go back to the window.*]
   And say to her—wait! I have a message for her.
   Say to her this, Giulietta: The foot stumbles,
   The hand hath its own awkward way; the tongue
   Moves foolishly in the mouth; but in the heart
   The truth lies, and all's well 'twixt her and me.
   Can you remember that?
GIULIETTA: Ay, madam, I think so.
   If not the words at least the gist of it.
BIANCA: Forget it all, my good child, but forget not:
   All's well 'twixt her and me.
GIULIETTA: Nay, that I have.
BIANCA: I will sleep now a little. Do you leave me.
   But go not far.
[*She lies still for a moment, then starts up.*]
   I hear the sound of hoofbeats!
GIULIETTA: Nay, madam.
BIANCA: Ay, I tell you! I can hear them!
   My face upon the pillow brings my ear
   Nearer the ground! She is coming! Open the door!
[*She kneels up in bed and holds out her arms toward the door, maintaining this position till* BEATRICE *comes.* GIULIETTA, *weeping, opens the door, and stands in it, shaking her head sadly.*]
GIULIETTA: [*Suddenly lifting her head and listening.*]
   Nay, it is so! I hear it now myself!
   Ay, there's a horse upon the bridge!
BIANCA: She's coming!
   Stand back! Stand out of the doorway!
[*Pause.*]
SERVANT: [*Entering.*] Majesty,

The Queen is here.

BIANCA: Ay, ay! Stand out of the doorway!

[*Pause.*]

GIULIETTA: She is here! She is in the court! She has leaped from horse!
Madam, oh, God be praised! This way!

BIANCA: Sister!

[BEATRICE *enters in her riding clothes, leaps to the bed.* BIANCA *throws her arms about her neck, and dies.*]

BEATRICE: [*After a moment, looking down at her.*]
Snow-White! Oh, no! Oh, no! Snow-White!

[*She screams.*]
Ah-h! Help me!
She is dying!

[*Attendants and nurses rush in, also the children.*]

LITTLE SNOW-WHITE: Mother, wake up!

LITTLE ROSE-RED: Finish the story!

BEATRICE: Take them away. Snow-White! [*Leaning over the bed.*]

NURSE: Nay, it is over, madam.

BEATRICE: Leave me. Leave me alone with her.

[*Exeunt all but* BEATRICE. *She kneels beside the bed*]

Scene V

A room at Lagoverde. The next day. BEATRICE *alone.*

BEATRICE: In sooth, I do not feel the earth so firm
Under my feet as yesterday it was.
All that I loved are gone to a far land,
And left me here alone, save for two children
And twenty thousand enemies, and the thing
Of horror that's in store for me. Almost
I feel my feet uprooted from the earth,
There's such a tugging at me to be gone.
Save for your children [*looking off stage toward* BIANCA'S *room*] 'twould
be simple enough
To lay me down beside you in your bed,
And call on Death, who is not yet out of hearing,
To take me, too.

Enter FIDELIO.

FIDELIO: Mistress, I have news for you.

Guido is dead!

BEATRICE: Is dead?

FIDELIO: Ay, he is dead.

Dead of a dagger i' the back, and dead enough
For twenty. Scarce were you gone an hour's time
We came upon him cold. And in a pool
Near by, the Lady Francesca floating drowned,
Who last was seen a-listening like a ghost
At the door of the dungeon. 'Tis a marvelous thing!
But that's not all!

BEATRICE: Nay, what more can there be?

FIDELIO: Mistress, in the night the people of Fiori
Rose like a wind and swept the Duke's men down
Like leaves! Come home! Come home! We will have supper
On a flat rock, behind a mulberry bush,
Of milk and tarts and honey and white bread—
All in one day!

BEATRICE: There is but half of me
To hear your tidings. I would clasp my hands together
But one of them is stricken from my side.

Enter GIULIETTA.

GIULIETTA: Madam.

BEATRICE: Ay, Giulietta.

GIULIETTA: Madam, last night,
Before you came, she bade me tell you something,
And not forget. 'Tis this: That the foot stumbles,
The hand doth awkward things, and the foolish tongue
Says what it would not say, but in the heart
Truth lies, and all is well 'twixt her and you.

[*She starts to go out, and turns back at the door.*]

She bade me above all things to forget not
The last: that all is well 'twixt her and you.

[*Exit.*]

BEATRICE: [*Slowly and with great content.*] She is not gone from me.
  Oh, there be places
  Farther away than Death! She is returned
  From her long silence, and rings out above me
  Like a silver bell! Let us go back, Fidelio,
  And gather up the fallen stones, and build us
  Another tower.

  Curtain.

TWO SLATTERNS AND A KING

PERSONS

THE KING
CHANCE THE VICE
TIDY THE FALSE SLATTERN
SLUT THE TRUE SLATTERN
THE PROLOGUE AND EPILOGUE ARE SPOKEN BY CHANCE

TWO SLATTERNS AND A KING

I am that cunning infidel
By men called CHANCE, *you know me well.*
It is through me you met your wives;
Through me your harvest blights or thrives;
And one and all, through me, today
Hither you came to see the play,
Which if your favor still you lend,
As now, so on until the end,
You shall be taught what way a King
Though a sublime and awful thing
And even wise, may come to be
A laughing-stock, and all through me!

[*Exit.*]

Enter KING.

KING: I am the King of all this land:
   I hold a scepter in my hand;
   Upon my head I wear a crown;
   Everybody stands when I sit down.

[*Sits.*]

CHANCE: [*Appearing to audience; he is invisible throughout the play to the other players in it.*]

Excepting me, please bear in mind
I sit whenever I feel inclined.

[*Sits.*]

KING: Although my lands are wide and long,
My walls right thick, my armies strong,
I am not wholly satisfied.

CHANCE: That is because you have no bride.

KING: Who speaks? Come forth and, if you dare,
Say once again what causes my care!
Why I am discontent with life!

CHANCE: It is because you have no wife.

KING: A woman in my royal house!
A woman! A wife! A bride! A spouse!
Bold stranger, that is not the cure,
For a woman I could never endure!

CHANCE: Per-Chance tomorrow you will find
You have altered your imperial mind.

[*Exeunt* KING *and* CHANCE *severally.*]

Enter TIDY.

TIDY: I am Tidy, I have been
All my life both neat and clean.
From my outside to my in
Clean am I unto my skin.
Everyday into a bucket
My hands I dip, my head I duck it;
And if the water plenty be
I sometimes wet some more of me.
This is my kitchen, where you will find
All things pleasant and to your mind;
Against the wall in orderly pairs—
One, two, one, two, observe my chairs.
In the middle of the room my table stands:
I would not move it for many lands.
My basins and bowls are all in their places;
The bottoms of my pots are as clean as your faces.
My kettle boils so cheerily,

It is like a friendly voice to me;
About my work I merrily sing,
And I brush my hearth with a white duck's wing.
Oh, full is every cupboard, sharp is every knife!
My bright, sunny kitchen is the pride of my life!

[*Exit* TIDY.]

Enter SLUT.

SLUT: I am Slut; I am a slattern,
You must not take me for your pattern.
I spend my days in slovenly ease;
I sleep when I like and I wake when I please.
My manners, they are indolent;
In clutter and filth I am quite content.
This is my kitchen, where I stir up my messes,
And wear out my old shoes and soiled silk dresses.
My table sags beneath the weight
Of stale food and unwashed plate;
The cat has tipped the pitcher o'er,
The greasy cream drips onto the floor;
Under the table is a broken cup—
I am too tired to pick it up.

[*Exit* SLUT.]

Enter KING.

KING: Now I will no longer tarry
For I think that I will marry.
Now the one thing in my life
Is to marry me a wife.
But I will not be content
With a wench that's indolent,
Or take a slattern for a spouse,
I will go from house to house,
Unheralded—that there may be
No cleaning up because of me—
And that maid whose kitchen's neatest
Will I have to be my sweetest.

[*Exit* KING.]

CHANCE *appears.*

CHANCE: That I am absent do not fear
   For that you have not seen me here,
   For know, I oft invisibly
   Do move among the things you see;
   And to confuse and thwart the King
   Through Slut and Tidy, is a thing
   Dear to my nature, wherefore heed,
   And you shall see a show indeed!

                                        [*Exit* Chance.]

       Enter TIDY *in great disorder.*

TIDY: Oh, dear, oh, dear, what shall I do?
   Oh, such a plight I never knew!
   Though I arose as is my way
   An hour before the break of day,
   Here it is noon, and nothing done;
   The milk has soured in the sun,
   And the sweet, pretty duck I broiled
   A neighbor's dog has dragged and spoiled;
   I beat him with my hands and wept!
   Straight through the window then he leapt,
   And through the window after him,
   With scratchèd face and bruisèd limb,
   And on through mire and brier and bog
   Hours and hours I chased that dog,
   Stumbling, uttering awful cries—
   While into my kitchen swarmed the flies!
   I came back at half-past ten!
   Oh, what a sight did greet me then!
   My fair white sheets I'd hung so fine
   Down in the black muck under the line!
   And out of the oven from cakes 'n' pies 'n'
   Beautiful tarts the thick smoke risin'!
   I knelt down my tarts to remove,
   And my quince jelly that stood on the stove

Up did boil, and, as you see,
Boiled itself all over me!
All over the floor, all over the room,
Whereat I ran to fetch the broom—
The broom! The broom—instead of the mop!
To fetch a broom to wipe up slop!
And with its handle smashed the clock's face,
Getting glass all over the place,
And knocked the dishes off the shelf,
And fell to my knees and cut myself,
And wept and cried and when I would rise
Could not see for the tears in my eyes;
So tripped on a chair and, to save a fall,
Caught at the table, then flat did sprawl,
Dragging the table down with me,
And everything on it, as well you may see!
I cannot live in such a state!
But where to begin is past my pate!

       Enter KING.

KING: I am the King of all these lands:
Down upon your knees and hands.
Wishing to marry me, I have said
That the tidiest maiden I would wed
In all my realm, wherefore I go
From kitchen to kitchen, that I may know
And judge for myself what maid is worth
To sit by my side in feasting and in mirth.
Untidy Spill-time, it is easy to see
That my fair bride you never will be.

TIDY: Oh, great King, hear me when I say
This has been a most unusual day!
It is by chance alone you see
In such a state my kitchen and me!
I can set us both to rights in a minute!

KING: In vain! I have set a trap and caught you in it!

Vain, wench, your lies and your pretense!
I see what I see and I hie me hence!

[*Exit* KING. *Exit* TIDY, *weeping.*]

Enter SLUT.

SLUT: Lest you know me not in this disguise
I tell you I am Slut, and I tell you no lies.
My face and my hands are clean and neat;
Fresh is my frock, trim are my feet.
But I assure you you are not wrong
To think that so tidy I shall not be for long.
And if the story you wish from me,
I will tell you how this came to be:
Dull was the day and tedious my book;
I saw no pleasure wherever I might look;
I had done everything that I knew how to do,
And I could think of nothing new.
But at last I thought of one
Thing that I had never done.
And I said, "I will take a broom,
And I will sweep this room!
I will wash this floor!"
I had never washed it before—
"All things in order will I arrange,
Although I hate order, for it will be a change."
So here I am, as you can see—
I and my kitchen as clean as can be.
But in a room as clean as this
My bones ache and I find no bliss.
So watch, and soon it will appear
Much less orderly and drear.

Enter KING.

KING: Down upon your knees and hands!
I am the King of all these lands.
Wishing to marry me, I have said
That the tidiest maiden I would wed

In all my realms, wherefore I go
From kitchen to kitchen that I may know—
Yet stay! This kitchen is so tidy,
I think that you must be my bridey!
As far and wide as I have been
So neat a kitchen I have not seen;
Wherefore I say you are my wife,
For the remainder of your life.

SLUT: [*Aside.*] To point him out his error at first I intended,
But least said is soonest mended.

[*Exit* KING *with* SLUT.]

Enter TIDY.

TIDY: Now once again with me
All is as it is wont to be.
Now once again you see me stand
The tidiest lady in the land.
If the King should see me now
He would tell a different tale, I trow.

Enter KING.

KING: Oh, lovely lady, who are you,
That I am talking to?

TIDY: She am I whom you did scorn
This very day at morn.

KING: It may not be as you have said,
For you would I gladly wed!

TIDY: I thank you for the favor, but
They tell me you have married Slut!

KING: Oh, cock's bones! And strike me dead!
Is it a Slut that I have wed?

Enter SLUT *dressed as at first.*

SLUT: So here you dally whilst I sit at home!
Never anymore abroad shall you roam,
But sit at home with me for the rest of your life,
For I am your lawful wedded wife!

KING: Oh, woe is me, what a life will be mine!

SLUT: It is too late now to repine:
  Home with me you come for the rest of your life,
  For Slut is your lawful wedded wife!

[*Exit* SLUT *with* KING.]

TIDY: A slattern is a fearful sight, ah, me!
  What pleasure it gives so tidy to be!

[*Exit* TIDY.]

EPILOGUE

Now that the play is at an end,
By Chance you have enjoyed it, friend;
By Chance to you his sweet was gall;
By Chance you slumbered through it all.
Howe'er it be, it was by Chance
The King was led so merry a dance,
By Chance that Tidy met disgrace,
By Chance alone Slut washed her face;
From morn to eve the whole day long
It was by Chance that things went wrong.
Wherefore, good friends, t' escape derision,
Be not o'er hasty in your decision,
For he who heedeth not this rule
BY CHANCE HE WILL BE CALLED A FOOL!

ENDNOTES

INTRODUCTION

[1] Quoted in Milford, Nancy, *Savage Beauty: The Life of Edna St. Vincent Millay.* (New York: Random House, 2001), 93, 185.

[2] *The Poems of Emily Dickinson,* edited by R. W. Franklin. (Cambridge and London: Belknap Press, 1998), 163.

SUGGESTED READING

CLARK, SUZANNE. *Sentimental Modernism: Women Writers and the Revolution of the Word.* Bloomington: University of Indiana Press, 1991.

DICKIE, MARGARET, AND THOMAS TRAVISANO, EDS. *Gendered Modernisms: American Women Poets and Their Readers.* Philadelphia: University of Pennsylvania Press, 1996.

EPSTEIN, DANIEL MARK. *What Lips My Lips Have Kissed: The Loves and Love Poems of Edna St. Vincent Millay.* New York: Henry Holt, 2001.

FREEDMAN, DIANE P., ED. *Millay at 100: A Critical Reappraisal.* Carbondale: Southern Illinois University Press, 1995.

MEADE, MARION. *Bobbed Hair and Bathtub Gin: Writers Running Wild in the Twenties.* New York: Doubleday, 2004.

MILFORD, NANCY. *Savage Beauty: The Life of Edna St. Vincent Millay.* New York: Random House, 2001.

MILLAY, EDNA ST. VINCENT. *Letters of Edna St. Vincent Millay.* Ed. Allan Ross MacDougall. Camden, ME: Down East Books, 1952.

MONTEFIORE, JAN. *Feminism and Poetry: Language, Experience, Identity, in Women's Writing.* London: Pandora, 1987.

MOORE, MARY B. *Desiring Voices: Women Sonneteers and Petrarchanism.* Carbondale: Southern Illinois University Press, 2000.

THESING, WILLIAM B., ED. *Critical Essays on Edna St. Vincent Millay.* New York: G. K. Hall, 1993.

SCHWEIK, SUSAN. *A Gulf So Deeply Cut: American Women Poets and the Second World War.* Madison: University of Wisconsin Press, 1991.

WALKER, CHERYL. *Masks Outrageous and Austere: Culture, Psyche and Persona in Modern Women Poets.* Bloomington: Indiana University Press, 1992.

WHEELER, KENNETH W., AND VIRGINIA LEE LUSSIER, EDS. *Women, the Arts, and the 1920s in Paris and New York*. Intro. Catherine Stimpson. New Brunswick, NJ: Transaction Books, 1982.

Look for the following titles, available now from
The Barnes & Noble Library of Essential Reading.

Visit your Barnes & Noble bookstore,
or shop online at *www.bn.com/loer*

NONFICTION

Myths of North American Indians, The	Lewis Spence	0760770433
Napoleon's Art of War	George C. D'Aguilar	0760773564
New World, The	Winston S. Churchill	0760768587
Nicomachean Ethics	Aristotle	0760752362
Notes on Nursing	Florence Nightingale	0760749949
On Liberty	John Stuart Mill	0760755000
On the Nature of Things	Lucretius	076076834X
On War	Carl von Clausewitz	0760755973
Oregon Trail, The	Francis Parkman	076075232X
Outline of History, The: Volume 1	H. G. Wells	0760758662
Outline of History, The: Volume 2	H. G. Wells	0760758670
Passing of the Armies, The	Joshua L. Chamberlain	0760760527
Personal Memoirs of P. H. Sheridan	Philip H. Sheridan	0760773750
Personal Memoirs of U. S. Grant	Ulysses S. Grant	0760749906
Philosophy of History, The	G. W. F. Hegel	0760757631
Plato and Platonism	Walter Pater	0760765472
Political Economy for Beginners	Millicent Garrett Fawcett	0760754977
Politics	Aristotle	0760768935
Poor Richard's Almanack	Benjamin Franklin	0760762015
Pragmatism	William James	0760749965
Praise of Folly, The	Desiderius Erasmus	0760757607
Principia Ethica	G. E. Moore	0760765464
Principle of Relativity	Alfred North Whitehead	0760765219
Principles of Political Economy and Taxation, The	David Ricardo	0760765367
Problems of Philosophy, The	Bertrand Russell	076075604X
Recollections and Letters	Robert E. Lee	0760759197
Relativity	Albert Einstein	0760759219
Rights of Man, The	Thomas Paine	0760755019
Rough Riders, The	Theodore Roosevelt	0760755760
Russia and Its Crisis	Paul Miliukov	0760768633
Science and Method	Henri Poincare	0760755868
Second Treatise of Government, The	John Locke	0760760950
Sense of Beauty, The	George Santayana	0760770425
Shakespearean Tragedy	A. C. Bradley	0760771693
Social Contract, The	Jean-Jacques Rousseau	0760770212
Subjection of Women, The	John Stuart Mill	076077174X
Tenting on the Plains	Elizabeth B. Custer	0760773718
Theory of Moral Sentiments, The	Adam Smith	0760758689
Totem and Taboo	Sigmund Freud	0760765200
Tractatus Logico-Philosophicus	Ludwig Wittgenstein	0760752354

THE BARNES & NOBLE
LIBRARY OF ESSENTIAL READING

This newly developed series has been established to provide affordable access to books of literary, academic, and historic value—works of both well-known writers and those who deserve to be rediscovered. Selected and introduced by scholars and specialists with an intimate knowledge of the works, these volumes present complete, original texts in a modern, readable typeface—welcoming a new generation of readers to influential and important books of the past. With more than 100 titles already in print and more than 100 forthcoming, the Library of Essential Reading offers an unrivaled variety of thought, scholarship, and entertainment. Best of all, these handsome and durable paperbacks are priced to be exceptionally affordable. For a full list of titles, visit *www.bn.com/loer*.